'Enda Larkin has ... with a foolproof, step-by step man ... rising of the so-called leadership gurus and ... actical terms, how to be ready to lead.'

Patrick M Delaney, Managing Director, Ovation Global DMC

'*Ready to Lead?* is an ideal companion for anybody starting out in an organisation which is results driven and recognizes the role of teams, large and small, in delivering sustained performance.'

Tony Kelly, Director of ICG

'Clear language, relevant case studies and a studied avoidance of hyperbole and jargon make this book an excellent companion for the aspiring leaders of tomorrow.'

Pádraic Gilligan, Marketing Director, MCI Dublin

'*Ready to Lead?* is a refreshing change from many other books on leadership in that it provides a pragmatic, practical and actionable approach to developing real world management skills.'

Mack Gill, President of SunGard Offshore Services

'*Ready To Lead?* is an invaluable and practical guide for anyone who wants to understand the difference between managing and leading, and use that knowledge to climb the corporate ladder.'

Richard Curran, Deputy Editor, The Sunday Business Post

'Practical, enormously helpful and wonderfully well organized!! The self assessment exercises alone are an important linkage to effective leadership. Enda Larkin has added a valuable, practical work to the expanding literature surrounding the topic of leadership. *Ready to Lead?* provides an effective guide to help maximize the reader's individual potential as a leader at all levels within any type of organization.'

James B. Hayes, Chairman of the Board Ashworth, Inc. and Retired Publisher FORTUNE Magazine

'Stop, think and question is a reflective technique for any leader, or aspiring leader and is well expounded in this book by Enda Larkin.'

Jim Coyle, Standards and Qualifications Director, ...

Ready to Lead?

ENDA LARKIN

Ready to Lead?

Prepare to think and act like a successful leader

PEARSON
Prentice Hall
BUSINESS

Harlow, England • London • New York • Boston • San Francisco • Toronto • Sydney • Singapore • Hong Kong
Tokyo • Seoul • Taipei • New Delhi • Cape Town • Madrid • Mexico City • Amsterdam • Munich • Paris • Milan

PEARSON EDUCATION LIMITED

Edinburgh Gate
Harlow CM20 2JE
Tel: +44 (0)1279 623623
Fax: +44 (0)1279 431059
Website: www.pearsoned.co.uk

First published in Great Britain in 2008

ISBN: 978-0-273-71506-1

British Library Cataloguing-in-Publication Data
A catalogue record for this book is available from the British Library

Library of Congress Cataloging-in-Publication Data
Larkin, Enda M.
    Ready to lead? : prepare to think and act like a successful leader / Enda M. Larkin.
        p. cm.
    Includes index.
    ISBN 978-0-273-71506-1
    1. Leadership--Handbooks, manuals, etc. 2. Management--Handbooks, manuals, etc. I. Title.
    HD57.7.L37 2008
    658.4'092--dc22   2007036510

10 9 8 7 6 5 4 3 2 1
11 10 09 08 07

Typeset in 9.5/14.5pt IowanOldSt BT by 3
Printed and bound in Great Britain by Henry Ling Ltd, Dorchester, Dorset

The Publisher's policy is to use paper manufactured from sustainable forests.

Contents

About the author

Enda Larkin is founding director of HTC Consulting and a respected consultant for public and private sector clients in Ireland, the United Kingdom, mainland Europe and the Middle East. He has designed and delivered many leadership development programmes and specialises in coaching young leaders to maximise their potential. With a background in hotel management, he holds a BSc in management from Trinity College Dublin and an MBA from ESCP-EAP Paris. He currently lives in Geneva, Switzerland.

Preface

This is a book for people making, or considering, a first step into leadership. It is the result of over 15 years' experience helping first-time leaders to make that transition and is born from an understanding that every one of them found it a daunting prospect. All first-time leaders need support, which isn't always forthcoming because the 'sink or swim' mentality still prevails in many organisations today. Even when help is available, first-timers don't always use it; for fear that it might be construed as a sign of weakness. Therefore, moving into a leadership role may not only be a little intimidating, it can at times feel a bit lonely too. Consider this book as a friend to accompany you on the journey ahead.

That word 'journey' is chosen intentionally, for although it does have a beginning, the path to leadership effectiveness doesn't have an end. Instead it is a process of continuous self-improvement. It is the beginning of that journey which is the focus here. Whether you are close to starting in a leadership role, or just contemplating it, this book will help you to get ready for the most important milestone in your career to date.

Your success as a leader depends as much on your attitude as it does on your approach, so the goal of this book is to get you first to think and then to act like a leader. In doing so, there are no quick fixes offered, for in reality there are none. If you were hoping to find some nice sound-bites and 10 quick steps to leadership, then you are probably in the wrong place. But if you want to achieve lasting fulfilment as a leader, through personal change, then this book is definitely for you.

Acknowledgements

Writing this book was my passion. For those around me as I did so, it was probably a pain. I would like to thank everyone who advised, cajoled and supported me as I was consumed by the challenge.

Thank you to my parents, James and Nancy, without whose love and support I would never have made it to the point where I had something worthwhile to say. Thank you to Martina for convincing me to say it and for all the time spent by my side as I put it down on paper.

I am grateful to Dr Tony Lenehan, Kevin Moriarty, John Power (Tactix UK) and many others for putting me on the right path over the years. Thanks also to all the first-time leaders that I have worked with over the years who served as my inspiration.

Finally, special praise goes to Samantha Jackson at Prentice Hall for her guidance and support in helping me to produce a work that will have real value for those who read it.

Introduction

" Leading people is a stimulating and rewarding experience. "

Leading people is a stimulating and rewarding experience, never dull or boring, and constantly changing from day to day. Becoming a leader represents a great opportunity for you, but it also presents many challenges. The content of this book will prepare you to face those challenges with confidence.

A realistic view of leadership is painted here, because making it as a leader will not be easy. But you can and will do it, if you are prepared to work hard at developing your potential to lead. Is it worth all the effort? Ask any successful leader and they will tell you there is nothing else in the world they would rather be doing. So the challenges ahead might be significant, but so too are the rewards.

You may already know the start date for your step up into leadership, or you might simply be considering it as an option for the future. In either case you are looking for support. If your move is imminent, then the topics covered here will prepare you to hit the ground running. If you are still unsure if leading others is right for you, then this book will help you to make that decision. Wherever you are on your journey, you will find lots of guidance as you get ready to lead.

As you look to the future, keep two important points in mind:

1 *Don't underestimate this step you are taking*

   Many experienced leaders look back at their first leadership position as having been the most challenging, from the point of view of coping with the many changes it brings. It's a big step – get it wrong and your future as a leader could end very quickly – so give it the time and attention it deserves.

2 *Don't overestimate it so much that it starts to intimidate you*

Some first-time leaders allow themselves to become overawed by what lies ahead. Remember, you are not being asked to fly the space shuttle to the moon, so keep things in perspective. With proper preparation, willingness to change and consistent effort on your part, you can make it and you will look back in the years ahead and wonder what all the fuss was about.

That word 'preparation' is the key though. If you fail to prepare, then you prepare to fail as the old saying goes, and in relation to your potential to lead, this rings particularly true. But where do you start when faced with such an array of characteristics, skills and techniques that must be mastered over time? There is indeed much to learn and plenty to do, so it is best to break the task down into more manageable bites. To provide focus and direction for your efforts, we will use a leadership framework comprising six stepping stones.

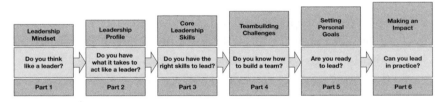

These stepping stones combine to give you a good head-start as a leader and they form the main parts of this book:

Part 1 – Leadership Mindset focuses on enhancing your understanding of leadership and the leader's role and explains why you should seek to lead, not manage. Here you will address the important question: Do I think like a leader?

Part 2 – Leadership Profile explores the personal qualities you will need to make it as a leader and encourages you to ask yourself: Do I have what it takes to act like a leader?

Part 3 – Core Leadership Skills highlights the core skills necessary to be an effective leader and requires you to consider: Do I have the right skills to lead?

Part 4 – Teambuilding Challenges identifies the components of a winning team and addresses common teambuilding issues. It helps you to answer the important question: Do I know how to build a team?

Part 5 – Setting Personal Goals defines the key goals that should guide your personal development efforts as you make the transition into leadership. It focuses on the central question: Am I ready to lead?

Part 6 – Making an Impact concentrates on your early days in the role and offers practical guidance on applying your leadership style and building your team. It encourages you to consider: Can I lead in practice?

There are lots of things you already know about leadership, yet there are still plenty of unknowns. The content here will build upon what you do know and demystify what you don't. As you progress through the book, you will be continuously challenged to assess your willingness and readiness to lead. You will also find answers to frequently asked questions on leadership, as well as numerous exercises to help you learn more about yourself. You should tackle them as you go, making notes for use later. It might be helpful to keep a notepad and pen handy as you read.

Ultimately, this book is about you and your future. The decisions you take here will have important personal implications, so reflect intensely on the questions raised and view the time spent doing so as an investment, not a cost.

❝ This book is about you and your future. ❞

PART

1

Leadership Mindset

Do you think like a leader?

'Before everything else, getting ready is the secret of success.'

Henry Ford
Founder of Ford Motor Company

Isn't it interesting how some people make it where others do not, even when they are similarly talented? In any walk of life, success comes to those who are focused, determined and passionate about what they do. Yes, talent is important, but on its own, it is never enough. Drive, self-belief and hard work separate winners from losers. Succeeding as a leader will be no different for you.

It is important to recognise that leaders at work are not super heroes; they are ordinary people doing extraordinary things, but what initially sets them apart is their mindset. They 'get' leadership, truly believe in it and under-stand why it is necessary today. Because of that, their approach is very different. If you really believe in the power of leadership and work contin-uously to develop yourself, then you too can thrive in the role.

In Part 1, the emphasis is on helping you to develop a leadership mindset and you will find answers here to important questions such as:

- ▶ What is the relationship between leading and managing?
- ▶ What does leading actually involve?
- ▶ What makes a leader different?
- ▶ Why do you need to lead?

You will lay the foundation here for your later attempts to build your lead-ership capabilities, so you should devote the necessary time to ask yourself: do I think like a leader?

CHAPTER ONE

Leading and managing: what's the link?

Have you ever wondered about the relationship between leading and managing? You will probably have given it some thought, because everyone in your shoes does. Is leadership a function of management, or the other way round? Are they complementary or mutually exclusive? Is a manager a leader, or a leader a manager? Such questions are common and although a bit abstract, the answers are central to building a leadership mindset. So, you do need to consider them, but we will avoid getting too technical about it at the same time.

❝ Is a manager a leader, or a leader a manager? ❞

Differentiating leading from managing is never easy because the distinctions are subtle and not so easily explained. Be assured though, they are not the same thing. You will no doubt have seen snappy little one-liners used before to describe the differences and whilst these are great soundbites, they do not really help you in any meaningful way. We need to be more substantial here because how can you ever hope to develop the right mindset if you don't know what leadership involves in the first place?

Therefore our focus here will be to explore the link between leadership and management in more concrete terms for you to work with. Leading and managing happen in organisations, so a good starting point is to define the purpose of organisations.

Understanding organisations

If you were asked to explain what organisations do, you would probably respond with answers like 'provide services', 'make things' or 'achieve profit' and you would not be wrong in any of these. Organisations are essentially about results and every business, commercial or otherwise, has a range of outcomes it wishes to achieve. These can be, depending upon the nature of the entity, a combination of profit, financial security, satisfied customers, delivering quality products and services and so on. Think of your own organisation and you will quickly see that some or all of these results are sought.

In achieving these outcomes, organisations utilise various processes to make products or deliver the services. People are the backbone of an enterprise and ensuring that employees are as productive as possible is also naturally a concern. Therefore, organisations are essentially about three distinct, but related dimensions of work: *outcomes*, *processes* and *people*. These are important considerations as we distinguish between leadership and management, so you should keep them in mind as you read on.

From management to leadership

As long as there have been organisations, there has been a need to manage people. The application of leadership principles to the workplace is a more recent phenomenon and has directly resulted from changing attitudes to work. Management and leadership are closely related, but very different at the same time. They are similar as they are both focused on achieving outcomes. They are different because of the approaches taken to getting there. Both management and leadership are concerned with the three dimensions; where the emphasis lies is what creates the differences between them.

Management tends to focus more on outcomes. It sees the result first, then the people, and seeks to 'push' employees towards the desired

" Management tends to focus more on outcomes. "

results or goals. That is not to say that all managers are bad people, for they are not. What it does mean is that they tend to show more concern for achieving the outcomes, with less emphasis placed on the people dimension.

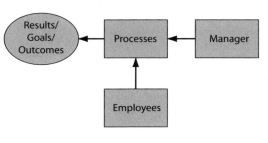

The way in which people are managed has continuously evolved. Go back in time and the further back you go, the higher the importance placed on outcomes and the lower the concern for people you would find. In fact, if you went back far enough, you would encounter a situation where there was no concern for employees at all. 'Old style' management approaches were based on the premise that the boss made all the decisions and employees simply did what they were told. This worked as long as people were prepared to accept it.

But you know that those days are long gone. Attitudes to work are radically different now and they continue to change. Consequently, the way in which people are managed has had to become more people-focused over time. As attitudes changed, managers were initially encouraged to develop and apply leadership skills as a means of responding to the changing nature of work. In more recent years, this has moved a step further and it is now accepted that people can really only be led and not managed. Today, the workplace needs more leaders and fewer managers.

Leadership places greater emphasis on the people dimension as a means to achieving the outcomes and seeks to 'pull' or attract employees to the required results, rather than simply push them there. Leadership in a work context is based on the understanding that if organisations or individual managers focus too much on outcomes and not enough on the human dynamic in today's work environment, this leads to significant problems.

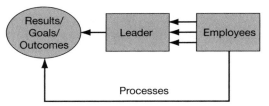

The case study below provides a good example of the effects of too much management and not enough leadership.

Case Study

One particular company offers cargo handling services at various airports. The teams at each airport are relatively similar in size and essentially perform the same tasks. Yet at two of the airports, the company found that despite a similar workload to all the other teams in the company, customer complaints were significantly higher, employee turnover was above average and delivery deadlines were often missed. In an attempt to discover the causes of the problems, the company analysed training levels, resources available and so on. Yet they discovered that these were all in line with those available to teams who performed well at other airports.

Further investigation through discussions with the employees revealed that the key problem at the underperforming centres was a direct consequence of a lack of leadership. At the two centres where performance was below the norm, 'old style' management approaches were adopted and it was very much a case of 'them and us'. There was poor communication, high levels of conflict, and these centres were operated according to the principles of management by fear. Consequently, in these underperforming teams, they found low motivation levels, higher incidences of aggression and generally a lower productivity rate than in other centres.

The two managers involved were reassigned and more leadership-orientated individuals put in their place. After this change and within a relatively short period of time, the performance levels rose and even exceeded the company expectations.

How many times have you encountered similar problems in your own working life? Sadly, all too often is the likely answer. This scenario demonstrates that when real leadership is absent today, this has negative impacts; on those who have to suffer it on a daily basis and for the organisation that allows it to happen. Now think more closely about your own past examples.

Action

Think for a moment of examples of poor management that you have personally witnessed or experienced in the past:

▶ What did the manager in question do, or not do, as the case may be?

▶ How did it impact on the employees involved?

▶ What were their reactions, how did it affect their interest in the job and the quality of their work?

▶ What was the atmosphere like among the people working for this manager?

▶ Did this poor management style impact directly on you?

▶ How did it make you feel and did it affect your own attitude to your job?

Keep a note of your thoughts for later use.

When you think about your own experiences, it is clear that your attitudes to work, your levels of motivation and your overall performance are heavily influenced by the quality of your day-to-day encounters with your boss. If you work for someone who lacks leadership, then you probably do the minimum work required. Whereas if your boss is an effective leader, your productivity is likely be much higher. This is not rocket science, it is simply human nature.

Leadership is based on the principle that everyone has a desire to work for someone who values and respects them. When employees feel that their boss treats them in a positive way, then the majority will give something back in return. People are not stupid; they can differentiate between leadership and management, even if they don't analyse it in a conscious way. But they can very quickly tell you how they feel when leadership is absent and whilst circumstances may force them to continue to work for poor managers, they do not bring their best efforts to the job.

People focused, but results orientated

A key distinction can now be made between leading and managing; leadership focuses more on the people dimension as a means to achieving outcomes. It seeks to attract employees to the organisation's goals, in a meaningful way, so that the work is done well not just because they have to do it, but in completing the work to a high standard employees feel they are furthering their own goals. Is it easy to achieve this? Of course not and nobody said it was going to be easy, but you will find that the results are worth the effort. This idea of having a greater people focus can cause confusion, so it is now important to clarify a common misconception about leadership.

❝Leadership focuses more on the people dimension.❞

Frequently Asked

From what you say, it sounds like leadership tries to create a holiday camp atmosphere at work?

You could be forgiven for thinking this because of the fact that leadership is very people focused. But attempting to create the perfect world at work is not the intention, nor is it ideal, or indeed recommended. This is not what leadership is about.

Leadership is not a case of the 'tail wagging the dog' for a leader is in full control, more so in fact than a manager, as they have achieved greater buy-in from their team. What leadership does seek to do is to focus on the team, as a means to achieving outcomes. Processes are still important, but the leaders recognise that they are only as effective as those charged with following them. A leader's focus is on the people because they understand that this will generate improved results.

Over time, effective leadership creates a situation where employees know what is expected of them, are involved in decision-making when appropriate, feel respected and valued, and respond accordingly. But they are also aware of the lines they should not cross.

Some important points about leadership

Being People Focused		
Does mean working hard to get the best from people	→	Does not mean forgetting about the required results
Is about motivating employees	→	Is not about pandering to their every whim
Does mean involving people	→	Does not mean relinquishing total control
Is about consulting with employees	→	Is not about conceding on every point
Does mean sharing decision-making	→	Does not mean letting them do whatever they want
Does require more thought on behalf of the leader	→	Does not necessarily require more time

The difference between leadership and management is therefore in the approach, for the desired results are the same. Leading has now replaced managing as the best approach. Nobody can predict the future, but one thing can be stated with a degree of certainty. The need for leadership will grow, not diminish in the years ahead because attitudes to work will continue to change. A recent study in the UK among second-level students indicated that one in seven had an ambition to become famous through an appearance on reality TV! Okay, this is just a light-hearted example, but it does show the different attitudes held. Anyone who thinks that people with such perspectives on life will respond well to simply being 'managed' is living on another planet.

&& The need for leadership will grow. &&

Leaders are different

In the past a leader was a boss. Today's leaders must be partners with their people. They no longer can lead solely based on positional power.

Ken Blanchard
Author and Consultant

If you saw a leader and a manager on the street, could you tell the difference between them? Probably not, but spend some time with each of them and you will quickly see it. Leaders and managers are set apart by the way they think and because of that, the way they act is very different. If you want to fully appreciate what makes a leader special, then you first have to understand this mindset.

The foundation stone of the leadership mindset is having a real desire to lead and being prepared to translate that commitment into action all day, every day. It is built on passion, self-belief and being fully in tune with human nature. Leaders recognise that they will get better results if their attitude and approach to their team is right.

Whereas managers view leadership as being one of the many functions they must perform as part of their management role, leaders see it *not* as a duty to be completed, but as something which defines them. This is an important distinction for you to understand, for it underpins everything a leader does. In practice, a leader thinks and therefore acts very differently from a manager, although they may actually carry out similar duties and tasks on a day-to-day basis.

Leaders stand out because they		
Think Differently		**Act Differently**
Recognise that attitudes to work today are radically different	→	Apply innovative approaches to bring the best out of people
Understand that simply telling employees what to do might be easier but it doesn't get the best results over the long term	→	Involve employees in decision-making when appropriate and regularly utilise two-way communication channels

Leaders stand out because they		
Think Differently		**Act Differently**
Realise that it is the people who ultimately achieve business outcomes	→	Strive to motivate their team, not just occasionally but all the time
Accept that people are all different and as such will not all act in the same way or respond to the same approach	→	Develop their people skills to a high level and have flexibility in their approach
Acknowledge that the past cannot be changed, only learned from and continuously look to the future	→	Have a clear view of where they are going which they continuously communicate to their team
Understand that the days of 'do as I say, not what I do' are long gone	→	Are role models for those around them – not perfect or infallible by any means – but continuously striving to be better

Successful leaders realise that leading people may not always be the easiest option, but it delivers the best results over the long term. As a conclusion to this chapter complete the following exercise.

Action

Consider a really great leader you have worked for in the past:

▶ What did they do that set them apart from other managers?

▶ What impact did their approach have on your performance?

▶ How did their approach make you feel?

▶ How did you respond?

Keep a note of your thoughts for later use.

How you think will determine how you act. Understanding what leading is and how it differs from managing is the first step in developing the right mindset. The following chapter will provide you with some more tangible reasons as to why you need to think leadership, not management.

As you get ready to lead, you must:	
Stop	**Start**
Thinking management	Living leadership
Viewing leadership as something to be done	Seeing leadership as something that defines you
Expecting that you can 'push' people towards outcomes today	Building your capabilities and skills so that you can attract them to the outcomes

CHAPTER TWO

The need to lead

How many really great leaders did you identify in the last exercise? Hopefully, you have worked for at least one in the past. If you did, then that experience will stick in your mind, because it always stands out. Unfortunately, effective leaders at work are all too rare. Leadership has become a bit of a buzzword in some organisations, often talked about, but not always applied in a meaningful and consistent way. Pick any randomly selected group of managers and very few will disagree with the principles of leadership, but only a minority will translate their words into action. You should set a goal for yourself now that whatever you do, you will not become a lip-server to leadership.

Part of the reason why leadership is not more widely embraced is that there are some myths surrounding the concept, which can cloud its real importance and prevent its application. We will address these here and provide you with concrete reasons as to why you need to lead.

Ignore the leadership myths

One of the most frequent misconceptions about leadership is that it only really applies to those at the top of the organisation. Given that much of the hype surrounding leadership focuses on charismatic CEOs, or senior managers transforming organisations, it would not be a surprise if you were thinking that way too. Go to any bookstore and you will find lots of 'how to' leadership books written by well-known senior business executives, but not too many written by 'John the guy who leads the sales team'.

So it is not unusual for people to think that the need to lead lies only at the top. But this is a mistake and here's why.

When you look at how your own organisation works in practice, there is clear evidence that the need for real leadership also lies further down the chain of command. Think about it for a moment. The senior manager in your business doesn't interact with the majority of the employees on an ongoing basis. Instead they deal through other managers, who are more likely to be committed to the organisation or at least to their own career progression and therefore easier to lead.

> **The need for real leadership also lies further down the chain of command.**

You, on the other hand, will be closer to the front-line and will have to deal directly with employees, whose commitment and motivation are unlikely to be anywhere near the level seen in managers. As such, you will have the tougher job in getting the best from them and as a result the need for you to lead will be greater day to day. Keep that important point in mind.

A second misconception about leadership arises because of the fact that great leaders are still in the minority. Many people in a similar position to you raise an important question.

Frequently Asked

I've seen lots of terrible managers and they seem to do just fine. Why should I bother trying to be a leader?

It's a fair point and this issue has caused many a heated debate on leadership courses over the years. Yes, there are indeed plenty of poor and even downright nasty managers out there who seem to get on just fine. However, to really address this issue in a meaningful way, you have to consider what is meant by 'doing just fine'. Poor managers can get the job done and often they survive over the long term, but when defining success, there is a major difference between *job done* and *job done well*.

Your own experience tells you that when you worked for a poor manager in the past, you did the job because you had to. But you did not put your heart and soul into it. On the other hand, when you worked for that great leader you identified earlier, you probably had increased motivation and consequently worked more efficiently and to a higher standard.

Also, there is usually higher employee turnover under the poor manager and this is a hidden cost to organisations. So they might survive, but they're not adding the value they could.

Keep in mind that the real test of effectiveness is not what happens when the manager is present but what goes on when they are not around. When poor managers are away for the day, you watch what happens in their absence. Their employees take what can best be called 'mental health' days and the primary focus for that time period when the boss is away is to simply enjoy their absence. This does not happen when leaders are out of sight.

When you examine the outputs between those who work for leaders against those working for poor managers, you can clearly see the difference in the two groups.

Those who work for leaders:	Those who work for poor managers:
▶ Are more productive	▶ Do the job because they have to
▶ Produce higher-quality work	▶ Work to the minimum standard
▶ Are more motivated	▶ Are usually unhappy in their work
▶ Go that extra mile	▶ Only do what is required
▶ Embrace change and take on new challenges readily	▶ Fear change in case it means extra work
▶ Operate in an environment based on trust and mutual respect	▶ Operate in an environment based on fear and suspicion
▶ Work together as a team to support their leader	▶ Work together as a team to survive their manager
▶ Learn from their mistakes and strive to be better next time	▶ Are punished for mistakes and strive not to be caught next time
▶ Look forward to coming to work	▶ Look forward to going home
▶ Are aiming for shared future goals	▶ Are aiming for a future elsewhere

These are not just clichés – they are real and tangible benefits that result from leading not managing. Do not allow common myths about leadership to distract you from your goal of becoming a great leader. Leadership does apply directly to you and although not everyone chooses that path, those who do see substantial personal and work-related rewards.

Grasp the leadership realities

Here are some more practical reasons why you need to lead. An initial point to consider here is that if you only view your role from a management perspective, then you are in danger of believing that it is your position that will give you your source of power and authority. This will be a miscalculation, for in today's workplace, real and lasting respect derives not solely from your title, but through what can be called your personal power. Your team will only respect you for who you are, how you react in given situations and how you relate to them on a day-to-day basis. In simple terms, those who think 'management' tend to over-rely on their position for their source of authority. Those who think 'leadership' use their personal power as their main resource.

> *Reality 1*
>
> *You need to lead because you can only generate real respect through using your personal power.*
>
> It is only through thinking and acting as a leader that you will begin to generate real respect and build the trust of your team.

Whether or not you think of yourself as a leader is perhaps irrelevant, because that is how your team members will view you, although they may never actually use the word 'leader' when describing you. But when things go wrong, who will they come to? When they need support and guidance who will they turn to? When the team doesn't function effectively, who will they blame? When it comes to the world of work, you will be at the centre of your team's universe for a certain number of hours every day. Although your boss may judge you primarily on your ability to plan, organise, control budgets and other hard skills, your team are more likely to assess your performance on the softer skills associated with the role. In other words, how you lead them.

> **Reality 2**
>
> *Your team will judge you on how you lead them.*
>
> You must recognise that your team will judge you on how you lead them and not on how you manage them, even if they don't think in those theoretical terms.

Take an example of this in practice. You have probably sat with your colleagues at some point in the past and complained about one of your bosses – we have all done it. It is safe to say that your complaints about the manager in question were not because they were a poor planner, or bad organiser or weak in finance and so on. What you were probably unhappy about was some aspect of their attitude or behaviour – poor communication, lack of direction, no feedback, or aggressiveness. In fact, you complained about leadership-related matters. You should remember this when you step into a leadership role.

Finally, if you do not assume the leadership role in your team, or if you operate as an ineffective leader, then someone else will adopt the role for you. Think again of a weak or poor manager that you have worked for in the past. Due to their lack of leadership, 'informal' leaders probably emerged who were no doubt the more dominant employees in your team. It was these informal leaders who were really in control and it is likely that they tended to work against the manager in question.

> **Reality 3**
>
> *If you don't lead, someone else will do it for you.*
>
> Every group or team, of any size, needs a leader of some kind and if you fail to assume the leadership role, then someone else will step into the gap you leave open.

These informal leaders we just mentioned are interesting characters and you should watch them from a distance, as there are certain things to be learned from them. If you observe them at work, or more likely in places like the canteen, you will see that they are:

▶ Usually at the centre of those around them

▶ Good communicators with their colleagues, but often transmit a negative message

▶ Able to attract people to their way of thinking, their desired outcomes if you like. Unfortunately these are likely to be contra to those of the designated leader. In fact, one of their preferred outcomes is generally to make life difficult for that person

▶ Always looking for new recruits. When a new member joins the team, they are quick to try to get them onto their wavelength – this usually takes the form of 'let me tell you what it's really like around here'.

So, although they are a destructive influence, you can see in them the application of certain leadership qualities and skills and, as such, they are worth observing. It is also helpful to point out here that leadership can have both positive and negative forms and your goal should always be to exert a positive influence over your team.

By developing your leadership mindset now and from that building your capacity to lead, you are preparing for a successful future. The positive effects of leadership are self-perpetuating, so the more effort you put into developing your potential to lead, the greater the returns you will find. Remember, leaders are always proactive not reactive when it comes to personal development.

> ❝ Leadership can have both positive and negative forms. ❞

As a conclusion to this chapter, give some thought now to building your own leadership mindset by completing the following exercise.

Action

The primary focus of your thoughts at this stage should be to explore your personal commitment for wanting to become a leader. Think about:

▶ How committed are you to being a leader and not just a manager?

▶ Is it really something you want to do? Why?

Now think about your own mindset:

▶ How do you view the leadership role differently now?

▶ What kind of leader do you hope to be?

▶ What might you learn from the leaders you admired in the past?

▶ Talk to a few people in leadership positions that you know and trust to see what potential strengths/areas for improvement they see in you as a leader.

Keep a note of your thoughts for later use.

Hopefully, you now see the need for you to lead. If not, maybe you should think more closely about whether you are going in the right direction. Leadership is not for everyone and there is no shame in choosing a different path. You can still be a manager, although you will likely struggle with the people dimension today, if you only see your role in those terms. With real commitment, you can and will make it as a leader and the remainder of this book will help you to move towards that goal.

As you get ready to lead, you must:	
Stop	**Start**
Thinking that leadership is for other people	Recognising that leadership applies directly to you
Limiting yourself to just trying to get the *job done*	Focusing on how to get the *job done well*
Hoping to gain respect through position power	Striving to gain respect through your personal power

Reflect upon

Having a leadership mindset will be the cornerstone of your future success. The more you think like a leader, the easier it will be to act like one. As you move ahead, take the following key messages with you:

- ▶ Managing and leading are not the same thing, although the differences are subtle.

- ▶ Leadership and management differ from each other, not in what they want to achieve, but more in the means and approaches taken to get there.

- ▶ Managers tend to see the outcomes first and view their role as being to 'push' their employees towards those outcomes.

- ▶ Leaders seek to 'pull' or attract people to the results required.

- ▶ Leaders and managers differ mostly in how they view their role and it is this way of thinking that most sets them apart.

- ▶ The leadership mindset begins with having a *real* commitment to lead and being prepared to translate that commitment into action all day, every day.

- ▶ Leadership will have direct relevance to you, not just to the senior levels in your organisation.

- ▶ Poor managers do exist and survive, but there is a major difference between *job done* and *job done well*.

- ▶ Your team will judge you on how you lead them and not on how you manage them, even if they don't think in those theoretical terms.

- ▶ Those who think in narrow management terms tend to over-rely on their position for their source of authority. Leaders use their personal power as their main resource.

- ▶ Every group or team needs some kind of leadership and if you don't act as the leader, then someone else will do it for you.

You now understand how leaders think, so we can shift the focus to how they act. Part 2 will explore how leaders behave.

Leadership Profile

Do you have what it takes to act like a leader?

'The winner is the chef who takes the same ingredients as everyone else and produces the best results'

Edward de Bono
Leading Creative Thinker

When first-time leaders fail, it is often because they are not ready to lead and by the time they recognise this fact, it is too late for they are in the thick of things and quickly become swamped. Don't make the mistake of believing that once you start in a leadership role, you will quickly learn the necessary skills and with time and practice everything will work out fine. Of course you must grow into the position, but there is more to leading than just learning and applying the necessary skills.

You should view the leadership skills as being the icing on the cake. First you need to have the cake, the key ingredients of which are the right mindset and having a leadership profile – a range of personal attributes that support effective leadership. Without these fundamentals, seeking to learn and apply leadership skills is essentially a waste of time because you do not have the foundation in place to help translate them into action.

In Part 2, you will find answers to important questions such as:

- ▶ What personal qualities does a leader need?
- ▶ Why do you need them?
- ▶ How do leaders behave?

The focus in the following chapters will be on the personal qualities and behaviours that you will need to translate your desire to lead into reality. As you read you should continuously ask yourself: Do I have what it takes to act like a leader?

CHAPTER THREE
Leadership qualities

What was it about that great leader you identified earlier that made them stand out for you? You are likely to have judged them by what they did – their external actions and behaviours – and they undoubtedly had plenty of skills that you admired. But what you probably didn't focus upon was who they were inside. But it is this internal dimension which enabled them to do the things you liked. There is an over-emphasis on the skills of leadership, in fact they generally get all the attention. They are of course crucial, but you can only apply skills if you have the right personal qualities to enable you to do so. It's a bit like putting sports wheels on a clapped-out old car – it's not going to make the car go any faster, because the problem lies under the hood.

Preparing for leadership requires you to examine what's under your hood – have you got the right mix of qualities to build upon to make an effective leader? Leaders have certain personal attributes that help them to:

▶ bring out the best in others

▶ apply the skills of leadership more effectively

▶ build relationships with people

▶ generate respect and enthusiasm from those around them.

In this chapter, we will identify common qualities which underpin the leadership role, so that you can determine your current readiness to lead others. Before we do so, let's consider a frequently raised concern about the leadership profile.

Can everyone lead?

It's that classic question again – are leaders born or made? Some people believe that the ability to lead is something you are born with, whilst others think that everyone can develop their leadership potential. To give an adequate response to this question, we must think of leadership in different contexts.

« Are leaders born or made? »

In a general context, there have been many great individuals throughout history who seem to have been born solely for the purpose of leading. Yes, they learned along the way, but it would seem that they were put on this earth for a particular purpose. In this respect, we would have to say that some extraordinary people were simply born to lead. But our focus here is leadership at work, so you should consider it from a different perspective.

If leaders at work were only born and not made, then the pool of potential candidates would be very small indeed and most of us would have to give up now. But leaders in the workplace aren't expected to change the world and as such have a different emphasis. Therefore, when thinking of the work context, we should say that leaders are both born *and* made. The born aspect is related to many of the lower stepping stones in our leadership framework – you need to have some basics in place which you can build upon as you move into the leader's role. The made element are the higher stepping stones, such as the skills and techniques that make a leader effective, which can be more easily developed and enhanced over time.

Therefore to summarise, everyone with a real desire and some essential qualities can enhance their leadership potential over time. Of course, some will excel at it over others, as in every walk of life. However, without certain essential elements, you will struggle as a leader and no amount of leadership courses will save you. That is why we are placing so much emphasis on the leadership mindset and profile. They are more inherent and not so easily developed in the short term and you need to give a lot of consideration to these areas.

What do you look for in your ideal leader?

Defining common traits and characteristics of leaders is a challenge as each successful leader in the workplace is different. As such, there is no one set of qualities which can be held out as being the ideal model. There are of course common traits seen in all leaders, but it is dangerous to portray any single list as being the perfect set. For our purposes, we will concentrate on building a leadership profile that focuses on the qualities most applicable to you as a potential first-time leader. We will also concentrate on the more tangible personal qualities which you can more realistically develop over time.

What do you look for in a leader? As we build the leadership profile, a useful initial exercise is to determine the personal characteristics that you look for in a leader. Think of that great leader you identified in the earlier exercise and try to describe the qualities they possessed that gained your respect. This time, focus less on what they did and more on what *type of person* they were.

Action

Consider that great leader at work again and try to define their personal qualities that impressed you and helped them to gain your respect.

Keep a note of your thoughts for later use.

Now that you have defined some of the leadership qualities you personally admire, you would find that if you compared your list to someone else's, many of the qualities identified would be the same, for what we look for in leaders are common human requirements. Keep those personal qualities you have just identified in mind as you read on.

The leader's challenge

In order for us to explore what a leader is, it is helpful to probe more deeply into what a leader does, for they are obviously connected. A leader's main challenge is getting the right balance between the *outcomes* required by the organisation and the needs of the *people* or team. When we talk about outcomes, what exactly are we referring to? In any organisation outcomes can be described as:

For any commercial business, maximising profit is naturally a key objective. In non-profits, the emphasis may be on achieving financial stability. Either requirement is achieved by:

Outcomes

▶ Ensuring employee *productivity* is high

▶ Through delivering *quality* products and services to customers

▶ By operating the business processes *efficiently*

Your focus as a leader in relation to outcomes will therefore be to make sure that your team members are productive, complete their work to a high standard, and carry out that work as efficiently as possible.

On the other hand, when we look at the people or team side of things, what are we referring to?

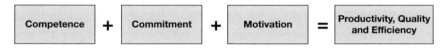

Therefore, in any organisation:

People

▶ Employees must be *competent* at what they do

▶ They must also be *committed* to the goals of the organisation

▶ They must be motivated to do the work to the right standard, as it is through this *motivation* that real quality and efficiency are achieved

This relates back to what we mentioned earlier about the difference between *job done* and *job done well*. Employees who are competent, committed and motivated are likely to be more productive and pay greater attention to the quality of their work than those who are not. In addition, overall efficiency is always higher when employees are motivated because they care more about what they do. So your role as a leader will be to ensure the competency, commitment and motivation of your team.

> **" Your role as a leader will be to ensure the competency, commitment and motivation of your team. "**

It is clear that the performance of the team and the delivery of the outcomes are interlinked and the leader's challenge is to balance the two equations. They do so by focusing on the people side first.

The Leader's Challenge				
People		**Outcomes**		
Competence + Commitment + Motivation	→	Productivity + Quality + Efficiency	→	Profitability/ Financial Stability

Leadership qualities

Now imagine yourself in a leadership position and consider how you will balance this equation:

▶ How will you get people to want to be more competent at what they do?

▶ How are you going to make them more committed?

▶ How will you get them to be more motivated?

▶ How will you make them more productive?

▶ How will you convince your team to be concerned about the quality of their work?

▶ How will you encourage them to be more efficient?

You will quickly recognise that you cannot force people to do any of those things. If you want to make these things happen, then your team will first have to respect you as leader. In fact, you will find the answer to balancing the outcome–people relationship lies within yourself. If you have the right personal qualities, then people will be drawn to you and from that they will be willing to be more competent, committed and motivated, which in turn will lead to greater productivity, quality and efficiency. Let's simplify this outcome–people relationship further, so that we can identify the type of qualities we are talking about.

Think of the outcome–people relationship as being two sides of a river, with the outcomes on one side and the people on the other. Your role as leader will be to bridge the gap by attracting the team across the river to reach the outcomes. You could simply force them across, as in the old-style management approach, but the likelihood today is that the more you try to force employees to the outcomes, the more they will resist.

Based on this simple analogy, you must have personal qualities that attract others as well as those that enable you to serve as a bridge between the often conflicting goals of the organisation and the team. You will therefore require both *attracting* and *bridging qualities*.

Leadership Profile	
Attracting Qualities	**Bridging Qualities**
▶ Commitment ▶ Self motivated/Energy/Enthusiasm ▶ Self-control ▶ Consistency ▶ Knowledgeable & competent ▶ Approachability ▶ X-Factor qualities	▶ Concern for others ▶ Empathy ▶ Open & honest ▶ Being supportive

If you look at these qualities and compare them to the list you made earlier, it is highly probable that many of the points overlap. The *attracting* qualities draw others to you. Again, you do not have to be Einstein to figure that out; people prefer to work for someone who is motivated, consistent and competent at what they do. They like someone who brings energy and commitment to the role and has an ability to remain calm under pressure. They also need to feel that you are approachable. Then there is the X-Factor, which we will come to later. On the other hand, the *bridging* qualities of a leader describe the personal characteristics that will support you in trying to build relationships with your team; having a concern for them, being able to empathise with people, being open and honest and supportive when the need arises.

If you have a good mix of these qualities, then people will respect you and you will be in a better position to balance the outcome–people relationship more easily. Simply put:

Balancing the Equation		
What you want to achieve		**The type of person you need to be**
If you want your team to be competent at what they do	→	You need to set an example by being knowledgeable and competent at what you do
If you want your team to be committed	→	They need to see real commitment coming from you
If you want to motivate your team	→	You have to be motivated yourself and have a concern for them
If you want your team to be productive	→	They will need to see lots of energy and enthusiasm coming from you
If you want to be able to deal with people in a positive way	→	Then you need to have the ability to remain calm and in control

A major part of your ability to meet the leadership challenge will stem from your own personal qualities. Anyone can learn skills, but without some of these qualities you cannot make them stick. If you don't have them, is that the end?

Frequently Asked

What if I don't have all these qualities?

Don't despair is the quick answer. Even if you haven't ident-ified with every quality on the list, you should not think of it as a catalogue of items to be ticked off individually. It is unlikely that any one of us would be blessed with all these qualities in equal amounts.

What you should try to do, based upon this list and your own consideration of the leadership traits you admire, is to build up a general profile of an effective leader.

It is against this overall profile that you should assess yourself and not necessarily by thinking about every individual quality that any list might identify. As a conclusion to this chapter, complete the following exercise.

Action

Give some thought now to your own personal qualities:

▶ Have you got the right mix to help you become an effective leader?

▶ Ask others whom you know and trust in a work context to tell you what qualities they see in you.

▶ Summarise your strengths and areas for improvement in this regard.

Keep a note of your thoughts for later use.

You have now explored the first part of the leadership profile and have identified the key qualities that any successful leader needs. In the following chapter we will examine how possessing these qualities will influence your behaviour as a leader.

As you get ready to lead, you must:	
Stop	**Start**
Focusing only on leadership skills	Enhancing your leadership qualities too
Believing that leaders are born	Recognising that everyone with real desire and essential characteristics can enhance their potential to lead
Imagining that people will act a certain way because you tell them to	Realising that you will need to lead by example

CHAPTER FOUR
Leadership behaviour

How are leaders expected to behave? Do they have to be perfect? Of course not, but they should stand out from the crowd. All leaders are different, so naturally they do not behave in exactly the same way. However, because of their personal qualities, they do display similar behaviour patterns. To better understand these behaviours, we will explore the *attracting* and *bridging* qualities in greater detail to see how they will influence the way you must act when you become a leader. From that, you can consider how you will need to adjust your current behaviour to fit more closely with the leadership profile.

« Leaders should stand out from the crowd. »

Attracting qualities

Commitment

You are already aware of the need for you to have a personal commitment to leading others as a prerequisite to success. When you become a leader, you must demonstrate through your behaviour a real commitment to your organisation, your team and the agreed common goals. The way you act in this regard will influence the behaviour of others. When you first take up a leadership position it will be critical to quickly display this commitment, both to your boss and your team.

You will show your commitment to your boss by:

▶ Devoting the necessary time and effort to establish yourself in the role

▶ Developing a clear action plan for what you propose to do as leader

▶ Keeping them informed of progress

▶ Using your initiative without overstepping the mark

▶ Achieving the expected results.

We will discuss later how you will need to agree concrete goals with your boss, so that your personal performance can be accurately and fairly measured in future.

To your team, you demonstrate your commitment by:

▶ Explaining your hopes and expectations

▶ Clarifying what is expected from them

▶ Showing a willingness to communicate with them in a structured way

▶ Listening to, and addressing issues of concern to them

▶ Delivering on your promises.

There will of course be times when your commitment is challenged, but you must not let this show to others.

Frequently Asked

What if I don't agree with company policies or decisions?

Of course you won't always like or agree with company policy or certain decisions taken, but you must be careful not to let this affect your commitment. First-time leaders often make the mistake of intentionally or unintentionally letting their team know that they are not fully behind something the organisation is proposing. They say things like; 'I know, I don't agree with it either, but we have to do it'. This is a dangerous thing to do because if your team becomes aware that you are not behind something, then you are in trouble when you try to get them to abide by it.

So, even though you will not always be in agreement with what your organisation is doing, you have to project an image to your team that you are.

This is not lying to your team, it is just being smart. If you have no control over the decision, then you will have to implement it and this will be easier if you are seen to accept it.

If you find that there are many policies and decisions you don't agree with, then this is another matter and you would have to question whether you are in the right place.

Self-motivated/energy/enthusiasm

If you really want to succeed, you'll have to go for it every day like I do. The big time isn't for slackers. Keep up your mental stamina and remain curious. I think that bored people are unintelligent people.

Donald Trump
Entrepreneur

One of the distinguishing features of leaders is their strong personal motivation and high levels of energy and enthusiasm. They strive for excellence in all that they do and are a role model to others. You must become the living embodiment of your expectations for your team and serve as the benchmark for them.

Some people start thinking about work when they clock in, or after their first coffee; others think about finishing the working day before they even start it. Not you as a leader. You should begin to focus on work from the minute you start to get ready in the morning. This does not mean that you will turn into a nerd, or become obsessed about it, just that you will make sure to get the simple things right like your appearance and arrive at work mentally prepared for the day. You should also consider your personal health and fitness, because this will contribute to your energy levels at work.

It is through your own motivation, energy and enthusiasm that you will really achieve things. If you set the example, then quickly you will find that others around you will be positively impacted by that. The opposite also holds true, so don't be the dark cloud that enters the office every day!

Don't be the dark cloud that enters the office every day!

Self-control

This will be a critical behaviour for you to display, so we will spend a bit more time on this one. The need for you to have good self-control cannot be overemphasised, as it will impact on many other areas such as your ability to communicate or to be flexible in the styles of leadership you use. Successful leaders

▶ can control their responses and reactions

▶ have the capacity to exercise restraint in the face of difficult situations and people they encounter on a day-to-day basis

▶ think first and then act.

Leaders are not robots; they experience the same emotions as everyone else, but they are more in control of how they respond and react. As we explore this issue, what you are really asking yourself is: do situations or other people control my reactions, or do I?

Life, and particularly work-life, is about dealing constantly with diverse situations and people. The ideal is to be able to control how you react by making a conscious decision as to what would be the best response in that instance. The reality is different of course and most of us have, to a greater or lesser degree, automatic responses to different *triggers* that recur time and time again. You are probably no different.

Think of it simply for a moment. For some people it's a case of having a bad temper that is hard to control, for others it's being afraid or intimidated by different situations or people that force them to back down when they should speak up. It is important to emphasise that having a range of responses from time to time is not necessarily the problem. Repeatedly being unable to control your reactions is an issue. In particular, aggression will cause you significant problems.

People and situations will always make your blood boil and an inability to control your responses will lead to difficulties in generating respect from your team. You will also create an environment where people believe that they need to be 'strong to survive' and quickly you will see lots more aggression going on around you. Those who do not like being in such an atmosphere will leave and over time your work-life will become a constant battle. Aggressive behaviour is not part of the leadership profile.

Frequently Asked

I tend to be quite aggressive with people, but you need to be tough to make it as a leader, don't you?

This is not an uncommon assumption, but it is wrong. Being aggressive is not a sign of strength, it actually shows that you are insecure, a bully and lacking interpersonal skills. Of course, as a leader you will need to be firm on occasion, but aggressive behaviours are not the answer.

If you are currently the type of person with a short fuse and if you are honest with yourself, this will undoubtedly have caused you difficulties in the past. We are not talking about losing your temper now and again, that's normal, but frequently becoming aggressive is the issue here. Being aggressive is in itself a mindset and in a leader's role, such behavioural problems will be magnified.

On the other hand, if you are the type of person who avoids difficult situations, or allows yourself to be a pushover, then this too will have caused you problems in the past. Again lacking confidence or feeling overwhelmed on occasion is not the issue, but being consistently passive will lead to difficulties in a leadership role.

If you have a high propensity for either of the shortcomings mentioned above, then that just means you are human. But you need to change this if you want to lead effectively. Don't make the mistake of thinking that you can suddenly do so once you become a leader. You can't. This is where a lot of quick-fix approaches to leadership lack credibility, because they make the assumption that by following some basic leadership rules, all will be resolved.

What we fail to realise is that our ability to control our reactions is but one example of a form of *conditioning*. By conditioning we mean learned behaviour.

A significant contributor to the way you currently react to different triggers has been your upbringing, your family, your school and friends, etc. You have in fact learned to behave in certain ways and the quality of that learning has been influenced by the various environments to which you were exposed. Of course, there are other influences such as hereditary factors, but it's not all in our genes. In any case, let's not get too scientific; suffice it to say that your behaviour patterns are learned and you have been exposed to good and bad learning throughout your life.

So you are 'conditioned' to react in certain ways and you probably don't even realise what you do well and what you do badly. To become an effective leader, you may well have to undo some of this conditioning and in effect re-learn how to exercise greater control over your behaviour and reactions. Is this going to be easy? No, is the short answer. It can be done over time, but only with a strong personal commitment and concentrated effort over the long term. Start now by considering your current strengths and weaknesses in relation to your levels of self-control.

❝ You may well have to undo some of this conditioning. ❞

Action

Give some thought now to how you react to different situations and people. What have your dominant reactions been in the past? Think of situations or people that put you under pressure. Have you frequently regretted your reactions in the past? To help you answer this, think of the following:

Aggressive

▶ Do you find yourself in constant battles with others?

▶ When other people raise a different opinion to yours, do you actually listen to what they have to say or are you planning your attack whilst they speak?

▶ Do you often 'lose your cool' and then regret doing so when you calm down?

▶ Do you see everything in terms of winning and losing?

▶ Are there recurring triggers that set your aggression off?

Passive

▶ Are you very self-critical?

> ▶ Do you find yourself wishing you could speak up in front of others but don't?
>
> ▶ Do you back down easily when another person disagrees with you?
>
> ▶ Do you feel others 'use' you at work?
>
> ▶ Are there recurring situations that make you become passive?
>
> Keep a note of your thoughts for later use.

Consistency

We all suffer from inconsistency to some degree, getting bursts of enthusiasm from time to time which can fade quickly. As a start point, you must be consistent in your outlook and frame of mind. This can be as simple as the moods you display. Yes, you will have good and bad days, and factors outside of work can have an impact on your behaviour. But as a leader you will need to display an even temperament, as who wants to work for a moody leader? The case study below provides a simple example of where a leader represented a negative benchmark in this regard.

Case Study

In one publishing company there was a particular team leader who was responsible for a team of administrative assistants. The team leader was known for his moodiness among the team members, with some days being good whereas others could be hell on earth. On the good days, he would arrive full of life and raring to go whereas on others he brought misery into the office.

Each day as he arrived for work, a team member would look out the office window to determine what sort of humour they thought he was in. The result of this observation would set the tone for the day within the office!

Have you ever had to live with something similar in the past? It is an extreme case, but this type of thing does frequently happen. Just think about it for a moment. The daily life of a group of employees was largely dependent upon what mood they perceived their boss to be in, on any given day. What right does any one individual have to exert such a negative influence over other people? Absolutely crazy of course – and make sure you never end up like that.

The effective leader behaves consistently in all aspects of what they do and people like to work for someone who is steady across a range of dimensions. You will need to be consistent in your own performance; in how you deal with the individuals in your team, in your patterns of decision-making, and in how you resolve problems. There is nothing that team members hate more than an inconsistent leader.

Remember, being consistent as a leader does not mean that you will become so predictable that you end up being boring, but you must not be erratic in your behaviour or performance from one day to the next.

Knowledgeable and competent

On one level the reasons why you will have to be knowledgeable and competent on work matters are obvious. As the head of a team, you will be constantly expected to give direction and for that you need to be up to speed. You do not have to be an expert, but you will need to understand the various jobs that the individuals who report to you undertake so you can guide them.

Frequently Asked

What if I don't know the answer?

This is a simple question that crops up all the time. Being the leader will not mean having all the answers, but it will be about finding the best solutions – some of which will come from within the team itself.

That said, you will still need the knowledge and competence so that you can offer guidance and support, resolve disputes, and solve problems on a day-to-day basis. The more knowledgeable and competent you are, the easier it will be to generate respect among your team. But you can't know everything and it's best to be upfront and admit it when you do not. But make sure you find out the answer and get back to them quickly.

However, if you can't answer every second question asked of you, then you will quickly lose credibility.

In particular, your first few weeks in the leadership role will be important from the point of view of developing your knowledge base.

The need for you to be competent and knowledgeable will be important on another level too, for it will affect your confidence and hence your ability to exercise self-control. This is often overlooked by first-time leaders and here is an example to highlight what we mean:

Case Study

One first-time leader found that she was constantly aggressive when questioned by a certain team member about financial reports relevant to the job. At first, the leader in question put it down to the fact that she just didn't like that particular individual. However, exploring the issue further with a mentor, she identified the real problem: that this person was more knowledgeable about finance than she was, so the aggressive response was actually masking her own insecurity. Having identified this, the young leader asked for coaching from the company's finance director. Over time, as her knowledge increased, so did her ability to control her response to that particular situation.

When you have the knowledge, you will feel more in control and this in turn will have implications for how you behave. So make sure you are continuously learning and developing.

Approachability

It is fairly obvious that you will have to be approachable as a leader and your team will need to feel that they can talk to you about issues concerning them – at an appropriate time and in an appropriate way. Managers often make statements like 'my door is always open' and assume that their employees will see this as meaning they are open and approachable. But there is no point in the door being always open if people are too scared to enter, or can't be bothered to go in because they lack respect for what's inside. Leaders recognise that being approachable is more than just making time for people, it relates to whether they consider you worth approaching or not.

X-Factor

❝Charisma is the result of effective leadership, not the other way around.❞

Warren Bennis and Burt Nanus
Leaders: The Strategies for Taking Charge

Finally, when looking at the attracting qualities in the profile, there is also this elusive characteristic known as the X-Factor, which could be personal charisma or the ability to inspire others. Often it's something that's hard to put into words. This X-Factor component is perhaps difficult to develop if you don't already have it, but you should still give some thought to what is unique about *you*.

❝There is also this elusive characteristic known as the X-Factor.❞

Frequently Asked

I am not a very charismatic person: so can I make it as a leader?

Yes, you can make it. There is a widely promoted view that all effective leaders have to be charismatic or inspirational to succeed, but this is not necessarily true in your context. Yes, it does help to have charisma and if you do have it, then great – you should use it to full advantage. But remember, there needs to be real substance behind the charisma too or people will quickly see through you. In addition, do not mistake arrogance for charisma, as they are not the same thing.

In reality, leaders at work are not the all-conquering champions they are often painted to be. There are unique qualities about them, but they aren't always shining lights. If you're not very charismatic, don't be disheartened, other qualities such as strength of character are just as important, so you may have other X-Factor attributes that compensate.

Action

Spend a moment now thinking about what X-Factor qualities you currently possess and how you might use them to best effect.

▶ What is special about you?

▶ If you were trying to promote yourself to someone who didn't know you, what would your unique selling point be?

▶ Think back to past appraisals you may have had at work. What were the most frequent positive comments made about you by others?

Keep a note of your thoughts for later use.

The *attracting* qualities will influence your behaviour to the extent that people will be drawn to you. They enable you to lead by example and, in doing so, you will be in a better position to attract people towards the desired outcomes or results.

Bridging qualities

Moving on to the *bridging* qualities in the leadership profile, the points to consider here include concern for others, empathy, being open, honest and supportive.

Concern for others

It will be important for you as a leader to have genuine concern for your team members, for if you don't, they will soon feel it. If you are the type of person who notices that everyone around you is unhappy but can easily ignore it, then you will not be an effective leader. That doesn't mean that team members won't sometimes be unhappy, or that you will never have to make unpopular decisions, because you will, but having a concern for overall team morale is a fundamental part of the leadership profile.

Showing real concern for your team involves striving to create a work environment that is as positive as it can be for everyone. It will require you to get to know your team as individuals, so that you can define their personal motivations and expectations and then to use this information to help them to develop. It will also mean being tuned into the mood of the team and taking action when you feel that morale or spirit is low.

You won't always like everyone in your team, but you have to tread carefully when that arises.

Frequently Asked

What if I don't like one of my team members?

It is not very likely that you will feel the same about every member of your team – that is a fact of life. However, you must treat all of them equally and fairly, so you will have to make a real effort to make sure you do not allow your personal feelings to cloud your judgement about individuals you dislike. If they do figure out that you dislike them, then they will use it against you. Every time you have to tackle them about some aspect of their work performance, they will try to project it back on you by saying things like 'you just pick on me because you don't like me' which is a tricky one to deal with, isn't it?

We will address such matters in greater detail later, but for the moment suffice it to say that as a leader, you need to focus on an individual's performance, not their personality.

> **You need to focus on an individual's performance, not their personality.**

Empathy

Linked to the above point will be your ability to empathise with others, to put yourself in their shoes so to speak. One mistake we all make is that we expect everyone to act and think as we do, but this can never happen, as everyone is different. Being able to see things from the perspective of others will be an important bridging quality for you as a leader. In particular, this will have application with regard to cultural and religious diversity, and you will need to be in tune with requirements in this regard. Having said that, every individual, regardless of culture, colour or creed, wants to be valued and respected by their leader. So if you can empathise with others, then you are unlikely to have problems handling diversity related matters.

Openness and honesty

People expect honesty from those who lead them and your team will be no different with you. However, the realities of work-life will mean that on occasion, you may not be in a position to give them the full picture. But you should at least be willing to be forthright and upfront with them when you can. You already know that there will be times when you have to project an image of supporting a decision that you may not agree with, but this does not mean you are being dishonest; it's just a fact of life as a leader.

Being Supportive

Your team will continuously look to you for support and when they do, you should take it as a sign that they respect you and value your opinion. Most of this support will be work related and relatively easily dealt with. However, from time to time you may be faced with more complicated matters, relating perhaps to personal problems or internal conflict within the team. Some managers run a mile from this kind of stuff, but the leader doesn't, for they recognise that it will affect performance.

On the other hand, you do not have to become an agony aunt. When it is a matter that is beyond your remit to deal with, then you should not over-step the mark, instead refer them to the appropriate channels for support.

These *bridging* qualities allow you to tune into the needs of others and as a leader this will be critical. They influence your behaviour in the sense that if you have them, then over time, people will feel that you value and respect them and as such they will be more willing to follow you.

Where to now?

In defining the leadership profile, our main goal was to get you thinking of the type of person you are right now and how you will have to change your behaviour as you prepare to lead others. As we said earlier, the list of qual-ities and related behaviours provided here is not exhaustive, but they are the priorities from your perspective. In particular, you should focus on how these qualities can influence how you behave and make a conscious effort to start adjusting your behaviour now. Is this kind of personal change going to be easy? Absolutely not, but armed with a leadership mindset, you will now recognise that it is essential and can be achieved with real determination and perseverance. You first need to be very clear where you are now in relation to these qualities; then you need to define where your areas for improvement lie. The exercise at the end of this chapter will help you to do this. Later, we will look at how you can begin to work on these, but you must recognise that this type of change is not going to happen overnight.

You should spend time now thinking about yourself in light of what we have covered here. Try to be objective and, where possible, talk to people you know and trust to get an alternative perspective. What you are essentially trying to do is to learn about yourself, so that you can make a break with the past, develop your personal qualities, and adjust your behaviour to enhance your ability to lead.

As a conclusion to this chapter, complete the following self-assessment exercise.

Action

1 Give some thought to the leadership qualities and behaviours that you may already possess. The following self-assessment should help you:

Please tick the box under the score that you feel best describes you

	Exactly like me 5	Very like me 4	Some-what like me 3	A little like me 2	Not like me at all 1
1. I work hard to meet my commitments to my team mates and colleagues.					

	Exactly like me 5	Very like me 4	Some-what like me 3	A little like me 2	Not like me at all 1
2. Even if I disagree with a proposal, I am prepared to work with it 100% when a decision is taken.					
3. I am always positive and enthusiastic at work, even when I don't feel like it.					
4. I keep myself fit and generally have no problem getting out of bed in the morning.					
5. I don't let things at work get me down and always try to see the bright side of things.					
6. I am good at keeping my emotions in check and don't easily lose my cool.					
7. I don't have an explosive temper.					
8. I am not afraid to speak up even if I am in the minority.					
9. I don't avoid difficult situations, even if I am nervous about them.					
10. I am not afraid of public speaking.					
11. I am good at setting targets for myself and work hard to achieve them.					
12. I am good at what I do and have been complimented many times on the quality of my work.					

	Exactly like me 5	Very like me 4	Some-what like me 3	A little like me 2	Not like me at all 1
13. I make a conscious effort to keep up to date about trends in my industry and in matters relating to my job.					
14. I constantly look for opportunities where I can learn new things.					
15. At work, people feel they can talk openly with me and often come to me for advice.					
16. I often speak up on behalf of my team on matters that concern us.					
17. I like my colleagues and go out of my way to help them when I can.					
18. I try to see the points of view of others and not just my own.					
19. I am an honest person and always try to be upfront with my colleagues in a constructive manner.					
20. I notice when other members of my team are having problems and I make a point of helping them.					

Total:

Scoring:
76–100 : You seem to have the right qualities to support you as a leader
51–75 : There is a good foundation there

26–50: You have a lot of work to do to develop your leadership qualities
0–25: Did you score it correctly?

2. **On a separate sheet of paper, summarise your strengths and areas for improvement with regard to the leadership profile. Look particularly at your lower-scoring answers as this will give you some indication as to the personal qualities and behaviours that you need to improve.**
3. **Define some practical steps that you can take from now on to address these areas for improvement.**

Keep a note of your thoughts for later use.

As you get ready to lead, you must:	
Stop	**Start**
Assuming that your current behaviour patterns will suffice in a leadership role	Developing your personal qualities and adjusting your behaviour now
Allowing situations or people to control your behaviour	Proactively developing your levels of self-control
Believing that your past defines you	Understanding that your future will be what you make it

Reflect upon

Leaders stand out primarily because of who they are inside; it is their personal qualities that make them think and act differently. You can develop your leadership profile, but it will not just happen – you have to be proactive. This is your first big test on the road to becoming an effective leader. As you rise to meet that challenge, take these key messages with you:

▶ Leaders are born *and* made.

▶ As a leader you will balance the outcome–people equation primarily by who you are and how you behave.

▶ Certain personal characteristics are necessary to make it as a leader, these can be described as *attracting* and *bridging* qualities.

▶ As a leader you must show commitment to your organisation, your team and agreed common goals.

▶ Leaders always have high levels of self-motivation, lots of enthusiasm and high energy levels.

▶ Leaders are in control of their own behaviour and reactions. They avoid aggressive or passive behaviours.

▶ Being consistent in everything you do will be an important quality when a leader. Team members hate inconsistency.

▶ Knowledge is power and you will need to be knowledgeable and competent in work-related matters that affect your team.

▶ Good leaders are approachable and your team members must feel confident in coming to talk to you, because they respect and value your opinion.

▶ Leaders do not always have to be charismatic but there is usually something unique about them. Be clear on what makes you special.

▶ Leaders show a genuine concern for their team members, they can put themselves in their shoes and provide support when required.

▶ Leaders are always open and honest with their team.

Now that you know how leaders behave, you can move on to Part 3 to consider the core skills that will support you when you move into the leadership role.

Core Leadership Skills

Do you have the right skills to lead?

'The key to successful leadership today is influence, not authority.'

Kenneth Blanchard
Author and Consultant

Every skill or talent that you currently possess will help you in some way when you become a leader, but it is obvious that certain skills will come more into play than they have done in the past. The list is long, so we will concentrate on those skills that will be of particular importance to you during your early days as a leader.

Think of what you currently do in your present role. What are the primary skills you use every day? Obviously, you need to have all the skills related to delivering the required outcomes in the job you are assigned to. As such, you depend most on your *job-related skills,* which vary depending upon the nature of the work you do. When you make a step up into leadership, you will still need these and in fact you will have to master new job skills such as planning, organising, budgeting and so on as you will be responsible for team performance and not just for your own.

However, when you start leading others, you will rely more heavily on a different set of skills that underpin effective leadership. Balancing the outcome–people equation will require you to master the *core leadership skills.*

In Part 3, our immediate attention will be on exploring these core skills in principle and how you can use them to your advantage. In later chapters, we will concentrate on how you will apply them in practice. You will find answers here to important questions such as:

▶ Why is communication so important?

▶ How can you communicate more effectively?

▶ What leadership styles can you adopt?

As you explore these core skills, focus your energies on understanding the rationale that supports their application, because if you understand the 'why', then the 'how to' will be infinitely more achievable later. As you read, you also should continuously ask yourself: do I have the right skills to lead?

CHAPTER FIVE
Communication

How many people have you communicated with today? Unless you were sitting alone in a dark room all day, you will have done lots of interacting. Communication is central to human existence. The ability to communicate has already been an important skill for you in your career to date and as you step up into a leadership role, it will gain even greater prominence. Successful leaders are always excellent communicators and it is not possible to overstate its significance, for it will be at the heart of everything you do. You will have covered the basics of communication before, so the general principles covered here will not be new to you. More likely it will be in the application of these principles where you may find gaps which you must start to bridge before you make the transition. Our focus here will primarily be on how you improve your effectiveness when communicating directly with others.

The art of communication

You have probably heard the phrase 'the art of communication' before, but you might not realise just how difficult an art it is to master. Every day we see people around us interacting and assume that communication is happening. Sadly, we tend to equate quantity with quality in relation to how we communicate. But lots of talking does not necessarily mean lots of communicating. It can often mean the opposite.

> **❝ Lots of talking does not necessarily mean lots of communicating. ❞**

It is a fact that, for all of us, our ability to communicate is a greater area for improvement than we might think. Most of us believe that we are good at it and rarely does someone openly admit that they are not. But if we all have such strong communication skills, then consider the following:

▶ Why are there so many communication breakdowns in our daily lives?

▶ Particularly in a work context, why are there so many communication-related problems?

▶ Why are there so many misunderstandings and disputes?

▶ Why do two people often hear the same message, but end up with two differing perceptions of what it meant?

There must be something behind these and other similar failings and we need to explore the issue, so that you can clearly define steps to help you to improve your ability to communicate.

One of the difficulties that arise in relation to how we communicate is the fact that it is seen as a natural activity, one which we have being doing in one form or another since we were born. Even in the absence of being able to speak, you could still let your feelings be known as a baby! You do not get up first thing every morning and think, okay, now I am going downstairs to interact with my family at breakfast. You just do it and it requires little thought. That is part of the problem and our belief that communication is a natural process is actually one of the underlying causes for our collective shortcomings in this area.

In one sense, your approach to how you communicate is similar to how you learned to ride a bike; in the beginning, you found it difficult and had to concentrate and think about it a lot. But once you 'got the hang of it', you stopped giving it much thought. Now you just jump on the bike and off you go.

The same applies to what you do in relation to communication. When you were young, you spent a lot of time learning the words that helped you to express yourself and then at some point in time it became a natural thing to do and you stopped thinking about it. Now you rarely give it any real thought, unless it goes wrong and then you may think about it, but usually to blame the other party for the breakdown.

Elements of communication – content and context

How you currently communicate is another example of *conditioning* and you may have to change what you currently do, as a stepping stone to becoming an effective leader. This is not going to be easy, but it is achievable.

First you need to look again at the basics of how you communicate and then you need to link this to what we said earlier about self-control, for they are related. From that you can develop a roadmap to guide your improvement efforts. As you do so, we will primarily focus on the most common form of communication utilised by a leader at work, namely face-to-face interaction.

When you talk directly to an individual or group, you are in effect sending and receiving messages. Sounds simple, but as you know, this isn't always the case. To have real communication, there must be common under-standing as a result. When you look more closely at what's really going on, it becomes clearer why the process is more complex than it seems at first.

When you interact directly with another person, you know that the message is made up of three components: words, tone and body language. You might have been on training courses over the years where you were given a rule such as: any message is made up of Words 7%, Tone 38%, and Body Language 55%, or something similar. Whilst this is useful in highlighting the importance of the tone and body language, it is not really very prac-tical, as it tries to put something neatly into a box which may not fit

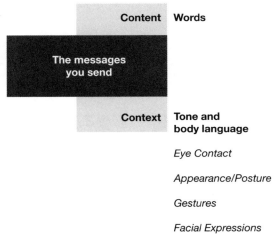

Content   Words

The messages you send

Context   Tone and body language

Eye Contact

Appearance/Posture

Gestures

Facial Expressions

on all occasions. Perhaps it is more appropriate to think of the messages you transmit as having two dimensions, *content* and *context.*

It is clear that the content of your messages is provided by the words you use, whereas the context is delivered by your tone and body language. Let's totally forget about percentages and say that to be an effective communicator, the content and context of your message must always be in alignment.

When you look more closely at the context of the message, you see that it is in fact made up of your emotions – how you feel about what you are saying. When happy, your tone and body language change as they do when you are sad, angry, hurt and so on. This is where the link can be made between your ability to keep in control and your effectiveness as a communicator. Here are two short examples of how context can overshadow content.

Reflection

Think for a moment of a situation where someone is angry and shouting at you. What they have to say may be valid, in other words, you may have done something wrong and be deserving of criticism. However, their tone and body language prevent you from receiving the message fully. As they are shouting at you, you respond to the context by thinking things like 'Who do they think they are?' or 'I don't have to put up with this' or perhaps you begin to adopt an aggressive manner back to them. In either case, you are not listening.

Alternatively, think of what happens if you are a very shy or passive person attempting to communicate. You may indeed have something important to say but because you speak too softly or appear to be very nervous, then you often don't get listened to.

In both these scenarios, the *content* of what is being said is not coming across, because the *context* is overwhelming it – resulting in a breakdown in communication. You have already seen lots of this kind of thing happening every day; if you watch daily interactions inside and indeed outside of work, you will see it is a regular occurrence.

Communicating more effectively

In seeking to become a better communicator, you naturally need to consider both content and context. Some basic points to consider when seeking to get the *content* right:

▶ Preparation is really important and the longer, or more important the interaction you are facing, the more you need to prepare.

▶ Even for short everyday interactions, be clear in what you wish to say and get your thoughts organised in your own head, before you open your mouth.

▶ Match the content of what you have to say with the requirements of your audience, be that one person or many.

▶ Consider what they need to know, what they know already, and how best to devise the message to make it stick for them.

▶ Be clear, concise and don't waffle.

▶ Be knowledgeable about your work and up to date with current trends. Take proactive steps to build your knowledge base.

▶ Avoid instances where you are put on the spot for immediate answers to complex issues. Naturally, there will be plenty of occasions where a quick answer is required and you will need to cope effectively with that.

▶ When you don't have the answer, don't bluff or think on the hoof. Be honest and tell them you will get back to them. Then make sure you do.

▶ Avoid overuse of meaningless jargon and buzzwords, or you could end up sounding like a walking cliché machine. Never feel that you need to join the jargon club – clear and simple is best.

In seeking to get the *context* right, things become somewhat more complicated, for a lot of what you are currently doing in relation to tone and body language is subconscious. Improving your self-control will help you here, as it will allow you to manage your emotions more effectively and therefore improve how you communicate.

The table below demonstrates how the three states of control influence our outward behaviours when communicating.

	Out of Control Being too shy or passive	In Control	Out of Control Being too angry or aggressive
Tone of Voice	▶ Quietly spoken ▶ Obviously nervous ▶ Overly apologetic ▶ Soft spoken ▶ Dry mouth	▶ Firm ▶ Calm ▶ Clear	▶ Loud ▶ Raised ▶ Shouting
Words	▶ Talking around the subject ▶ Avoiding getting to the issue/waffling ▶ Overly apologetic in choice of words ▶ Qualifying everything you say	▶ Concise ▶ No waffle ▶ Clearly expressing your opinion ▶ Using 'I' but in a non-selfish way	▶ Abrupt ▶ Threatening ▶ Accusing ▶ Using 'you' in a blaming fashion ▶ Swearing
Eyes	▶ Uncomfortable making eye contact ▶ Looking down or away a lot	▶ Maintaining good eye contact ▶ Not seeking to intimidate	▶ Staring down ▶ Eyes bulging ▶ Trying to intimidate
Hand Gestures	▶ Nervous gestures ▶ Fidgeting ▶ Hand wringing	▶ Open hand gestures	▶ Lots of pointing ▶ Clenched hands ▶ Thumping table
Body Language	▶ Inward posture ▶ Obviously uncomfortable ▶ Hunched, self-protecting	▶ Upright posture ▶ Head up ▶ Using active listening	▶ Forward posture ▶ In your face ▶ Leaning ▶ Threatening

Your inner emotions rush out through your external behaviour and that is why you need to work on your self-control as part of your attempts to become a better communicator. There is no easy answer as to how to do this, but a natural starting point is to be clear on where your current areas for improvement lie, which the exercise at the end of this chapter will help you to achieve.

The key message here is that to be an effective communicator, your goal should be to ensure that what you say and how you say it always complement each other. In terms of your external body language, the ability to make positive eye contact is of utmost importance for the leader, because it signals attentiveness, confidence and honesty.

Improving your listening skills

As well as thinking about how you send messages, you need to think about how you receive them. To communicate more effectively, you must be a good listener. Some people are terrible at it and, as a leader, this will be frowned upon by your team. In discussing listening, you should consider it from two perspectives; first, you need to see listening as a frame of mind and second, you must view it as a skill in its own right.

❝ To communicate more effectively, you must be a good listener. ❞

Operating with a leader's mindset, you must always be prepared to listen to your team members, individually and collectively. There should be structured communication channels in place, which provide you with formal opportunities to sit down and communicate with your team. In addition, on a day-to-day basis, you will need to make time to listen to the people around you.

You must also view listening as a skill to be developed, designed to encourage your team members to open up and to prevent you from doing all the talking in any given situation. We often assume that as we have two ears and don't have any hearing defects, then listening is not a problem for us. But it is very easy to be distracted by noise or movement, and our attention spans can be quite short. Becoming a better listener means using simple active listening techniques such as:

Maintaining eye contact

Obviously, this shows you are actually willing to listen, but it also helps you to read body language, which can often tell you that something in the content of what the other person is saying doesn't stack up.

Nodding

This again is an obvious sign that you are attentive and it encourages the speaker to keep going.

Encouraging

Simply interjecting on occasion with 'Yes, go on' gets them to continue to open up. This has less impact if you are not making eye contact too. Saying it whilst shuffling through your papers doesn't work!

Allowing short silences

Most of us hate silences and often try to quickly fill the gap. Don't be afraid to allow short silences to occur, as it lets the other person know that you are not automatically going to jump in and often this will encourage them to continue.

Paraphrasing

This means showing the person that you have got the gist of what they have said by saying things such as: 'So what you are saying is . . .'

Summarising

This means confirming in precise detail what they have said, to show that you have understood.

Active listening is about concentration and focus. Some people help us to do this because they are good communicators and make us want to listen. Others can drone on and drive us to distraction. In a leadership role, you must become a better listener regardless of the context that the other person uses for their delivery.

Work hard at becoming a better communicator, because it will be the key to your success as a leader. If you feel that you have a lot of work to improve your communication skills, you should consider taking specific training in this area. There are lots of worthwhile programmes available and it is such an important area in leadership, you will be glad you made the effort.

As a conclusion to this chapter, complete the following self-assessment exercise to help you to identify your current strengths and areas for improvement as a communicator.

Action

1. Give some thought to how effective a communicator you are at this time. The following self-assessment should help you:

Please tick the box under the score that you feel best describes you

	Exactly like me 5	Very like me 4	Some-what like me 3	A little like me 2	Not like me at all 1
1. I start every conversation with an open mind about the end result and am willing to change my viewpoint based on the valid opinion of others.					
2. Before I speak, I always think through what I am going to say.					
3. I always adjust my message to suit the person(s) I am talking to.					
4. I find it easy to listen to what other people have to say without interrupting.					
5. I am good at making eye contact with people when I am talking to them.					
7. I am confident when I talk to people and speak clearly without mumbling.					
8. I am good at getting my point across in a clear, concise manner without waffling.					

➤

	Exactly like me 5	Very like me 4	Some-what like me 3	A little like me 2	Not like me at all 1
9. I find it easy to concentrate on what others are saying and don't lose my focus.					
10. I don't start planning my response whilst the other person is talking.					
11. I don't think that my opinion is the most important in the room.					
12. I only speak up if I have something valuable to contribute to the conversation and I avoid talking just for the sake of it.					
13. I make a conscious effort to match my body language to the message I want to convey.					
14. I am good at reading the body language of others.					
15. I can keep my cool when talking to other people even if I feel angry about what they say.					
16. When other people in the group are quiet, I encourage them to contribute.					
17. I don't shout and point at people when we have a heated conversation.					
18. When group discussions get heated, I am good at keeping everyone calm and on the point.					

	Exactly like me 5	Very like me 4	Some-what like me 3	A little like me 2	Not like me at all 1
19. I feel comfortable holding meetings.					
20. I am good at summarising the key points of conversations that I have with people.					
Total					

Scoring:

76–100 : You seem to have good communication skills

51–75 : There is a good foundation there

26–50: You have a lot of work to do to develop your communication skills

0–25: Did you score it correctly?

2. **On a separate sheet of paper, summarise your strengths and areas for improvement with regard to your ability to communicate. Look particularly at your lower scoring answers and this will give you some indication as to what aspects of communication you need to focus on.**

3. **Define some practical steps that you can take from now on to address these areas for improvement.**

Keep a note of your thoughts for later use.

You should now understand that communicating is a two-way street and you need to operate on both sides of it. You must improve how you send messages, by aligning content and context, but you also need to enhance how you receive information by working on your ability to listen. In addition, effective communication with your team as a unit will be vital, as you seek to build and sustain a cohesive team in future. Having reflected upon the principles of how you communicate, the following chapter will explore the second core skill, leadership styles.

| As you get ready to lead, you must: ||
Stop	Start
Assuming that effective communication just happens	Working hard to improve your communication skills
Speaking first and thinking second	Planning all your communications
Allowing emotions to cloud your ability to communicate	Aligning the content and context of all your communications

CHAPTER SIX

Leadership styles

How will you deal with the diverse situations you will face as a leader? Can you apply the same leadership style for every one? It should be obvious that you can't, but what alternative approaches will be available to you? One of the most frequently asked questions by first-time leaders relates to what leadership styles they should adopt. There are many leadership theories that describe the various approaches that can be taken in accordance with some common principles. All the models are relatively easy to understand, but it is one thing seeing it on paper, quite another to be able to apply it into practice. That is where you are likely to encounter problems. Translating the various models of leadership in practice is a skill, it takes time to develop it and you will continue to enhance it throughout your career. In this chapter, we will explore a basic leadership styles model to guide you and later we will look specifically at how you might apply this in real life.

Leadership styles model

Fundamentally all leadership style models say more or less the same thing. They are differentiated mostly by their levels of complexity. All theories describe the styles of leadership on the basis of whether the focus of the leader is on the *outcome* or the *people*.

Early theories defined two polar opposites: the more outcome-focused the leader, the greater the probability that they were *autocratic* in nature. The more people-focused, the more likely they were to be *democratic* in their approach. However, this was an overly simplistic analysis, because it was too black and white. The realities of leading are shrouded in many shades of grey.

Later theories and models built on this basic assumption, but identified a range of styles. Some defined a sliding-scale approach from autocratic to democratic, whereas other models defined styles against a matrix based on the interrelationship between the outcome and the people. More recent approaches define styles based on different situations, or on the ability of the leader to inspire others by their actions.

As you prepare to lead, don't get too bogged down in models and theories. Try to grasp the general principles of leading in practice and then with experience you will get a better feel for the 'right' thing to do – bearing in mind that there is rarely a right way, only better or worse. To help you in this, we will develop our own model which is based on common principles.

The leader's challenge is to increase the competence, commitment and motivation of the team in order to raise their productivity, quality and overall efficiency. Based on this outcome–people equation, as a leader you will have to decide:

Outcome Focus

How much *direction* needs to be given to your team, or individuals within it and how much *control* you must exercise over their actions to achieve the outcomes.

People Focus

How much to *involve* your team in the decision-making process and how much *autonomy* or *freedom* to give them in the completion of their duties.

From this, we can start to build our model. Obviously, these can be conflicting perspectives *as* directing and controlling your team naturally reduces their involvement and autonomy. For example, when you provide more direction, this limits the involvement of the team in the decision-making process. Whereas, when you exercise higher control over the activities of the team, this reduces their autonomy to complete the work. Using these four elements – *direction, control, involvement and autonomy* – our model of leadership styles can be developed:

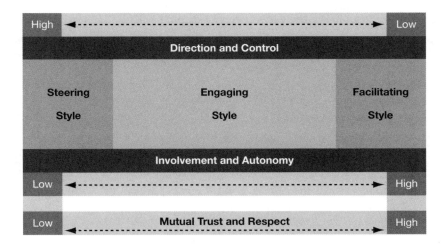

It looks a bit confusing doesn't it? But you will get the hang of it quickly and later we will look at how this works in practice. For the moment, just get a feel for the thinking behind the model. You will also notice that another dimension will impact on the leadership style you adopt, namely the levels of trust and respect between you and your team. As trust and respect grow, the nature of your approach should change.

So, as a leader, you will need to decide in any given situation and for every interaction with your team, or individuals within it, how much direction and control to exercise versus how much involvement and autonomy to allow. Based on this approach, three general styles of leadership can be described as:

> *How much direction and control to exercise versus how much involvement and autonomy to allow.* "

▶ *Steering Style* – This involves maintaining high direction and control over your team, whilst allowing low levels of involvement and autonomy. It is important to emphasise again that this does not mean being aggressive with the team, as aggression should not form any part of your toolkit. What it means is that you are more outcome-focused and less concerned with the needs of the team and are therefore taking greater control over their actions. This style is necessary where decisions have to be made quickly, or where a change has to be made which is beyond your control. It is also necessary during the early stages of dealing with a new team or with a new team member until they achieve the required standard. It could also be the style adopted when a team member steps out of line.

▶ *Engaging Style* – This involves increasing the involvement and/or autonomy of your team. This could mean including them in the decision-making process, or allowing them to propose solutions to given problems. It might entail different levels of engagement. On some occasions this might simply involve explaining decisions already made to your team – you may not be in a position or willing to alter the decision, but at least you are seeking to listen to their concerns. On other occasions, you would be consulting with your team about decisions to be made, or allowing them relatively high levels of autonomy in their actions. You always remain in control, but you are more people-focused using this style.

▶ *Facilitating Style* – This style involves allowing the team very high levels of involvement and autonomy of action. It is most likely you would use this style when you have a high-performing team where you play a reduced role, because you know the team can make decisions and take ownership for their actions. Mutual trust and respect would be very high here.

From our model, it is clear that you should seek to utilise the *engaging* style for the majority of the time. That is not to say the *steering* and *facilitating* styles are not used, but given the reality of teams at work, they are unlikely to be the predominant styles used over the longer term. It is also evident that as mutual trust and respect build between you and your team, there should be a shift away from the steering style towards engaging and facilitating.

Adopting a flexible approach

These styles are relatively easy to understand in principle, but their application is more challenging and this is where you will have greatest concern and often struggle with understanding when to use each one. The first response to these concerns is to state that these three styles are in fact part of a sliding scale rather than three rigid approaches.

In applying these styles, you are trying to be *flexible* in your approach by judging the best way to deal with each situation, or with a particular individual. On any given day, you could in fact use all three styles, depending upon what issues arise. The decision over which style is most appropriate will be influenced by many factors, such as:

▶ *Team Effectiveness* – When your team is well established and performs to a high standard, you are more likely to apply *engaging* or *facilitating* styles, because you know the team is ready for this. On the other hand, for new teams, or when you take over an existing team for the first time, you will have to utilise the *steering* style initially, as you must establish yourself among the team and get them operating to an acceptable level. This requires high levels of direction and control at the initial stages. Over time, as the team develops in the way that you want, you can then move towards engaging or facilitating styles.

▶ *Individual Performance* – Different team members will perform at varying levels and you must adjust your style for each. This change is subtle, but higher-performing team members warrant less direction and control than poor performers and require the application of *engaging* or *facilitating* styles more frequently. Equally, a new team member who is still learning the ropes will naturally require more direction and control than someone who has been doing the job for a long time and, as such, will require you to use the *steering* style.

▶ *Situations* – Different situations will always require the application of different styles. For example, when time deadlines are tight, you may have to use the *steering* style to ensure outcomes are met, whereas if there are changes required to work practices, this may allow for greater involvement of your team in the decision-making process. Here the *engaging* or *facilitating* styles are better.

In light of this, flexibility is the most important word. Easier said than done, of course, but with time and experience you will quickly recognise which style is most appropriate. This is what makes the application of leadership style a skill; it takes

❝ Flexibility is the most important word. ❞

time to develop and improves with practice. But remember, you cannot be flexible if you haven't already addressed the issues we discussed earlier, such as your ability to be in control or to communicate effectively.

As a conclusion to this chapter, try to broadly understand the three styles by reflecting upon what they are intended to do.

Action

Give some thought to how these styles might apply in real life. Answer the following questions for yourself.

Steering style

▶ What does this style mean to you?

▶ What are the different situations where you might use this style?

▶ Think of a past situation at work where you witnessed this style being used by your boss.

▶ Now think of a situation where this style should have been used but wasn't.

▶ What were the implications of that?

Engaging style

▶ What does this style mean to you?

▶ What are the different situations where you might use this style?

▶ Think of a past situation at work where you witnessed this style being used by your boss.

▶ Now think of a situation where this style should have been used but wasn't.

▶ What were the implications of that?

Facilitating style

▶ What does this style mean to you?

▶ What are the different situations where you might use this style?

▶ Think of a past situation at work where you witnessed this style being used by your boss.

▶ Now think of a situation where this style should have been used but wasn't.

▶ What were the implications of that?

Keep a note of your thoughts for later use.

In Part 6 we will use a number of practical scenarios which relate to real-life experiences at work to help you to more fully understand how to apply these styles in practice.

As you get ready to lead, you must:	
Stop	**Start**
Thinking about leadership in theory	Focusing on leadership in action
Worrying about all the leadership models and theories	Focusing on three basic leadership styles that you can use
Waiting until you start in a leadership role to develop your style	Watching leaders at work now and learn from what they do

Reflect upon

We have addressed two of the core skills you will need as a leader and it is important that you don't wait to start in a leadership role before developing them. In particular, be proactive in relation to your communication skills and watch and learn how other leaders at work apply different leadership styles. As you do, keep the following points in mind:

▶ Every skill you currently possess will help you in some way when you are a leader, but you must now develop and use your *core leadership skills* to a greater extent.

▶ Effective leaders are always excellent communicators. Two important elements to consider in face-to-face communication are *content* and *context*.

▶ Content is what you want to communicate; context is how you get it across.

▶ Leaders are always prepared to listen to their team members, individually and collectively.

▶ As a leader, you should understand that there is no perfect leadership style because there is rarely an ideal way of doing things, only better or worse.

▶ Flexibility in the application of a leadership style is the key.

▶ In deciding which leadership style is best in any situation, you have to consider between the levels of *direction* and *control* required, and how much *involvement* or *autonomy* to allow.

▶ This results in three key styles: *steering, engaging* and *facilitating*.

▶ The leadership style you adopt will depend upon team effectiveness, individual performance and different situations.

▶ In deciding which approach to take, you must become a thinker as well as a doer!

Now that you understand the core skills you will need, Part 4 will focus on some of the teambuilding challenges you will face as a leader.

Teambuilding Challenges

Do you know how to build a team?

'Individual commitment to a group effort – that is what makes a team work, a company work, a society work, a civilization work.'

Vincent Lombardi
Former US Football Coach, 1913–1970

Have you ever wondered why teams can be so different from one another? You will already have worked in various teams during your career so far, some of which probably functioned to a high standard, others not so well. Why does this happen? A lot of it has to do with the leader of course, but there are other factors too, which will be our focus here.

Most organisations today utilise the word 'team' in their descriptions of employees, but there is much more to the development of truly effective teams than simply describing them as such. You must recognise that effective teams do not automatically happen, just because people work in the same section or wear the same uniform. Even when a team has been working well together under a previous leader, this does not mean that they will continue to do so under your stewardship. Teams must be built, nourished and sustained; and teambuilding is a skill in its own right.

In Part 4, you will find answers to important questions such as:

- ▶ What makes an effective team?
- ▶ How do teams evolve?
- ▶ How will you motivate people at work?
- ▶ How should you deal with conflict?
- ▶ How will you handle change?
- ▶ How will you deal with difficult team members?

As you read ahead, try to relate the teambuilding issues covered here to your existing work team, so that you can apply the content to your own real-world experiences. You should also be continuously asking yourself: do I know how to build a team?

CHAPTER SEVEN
Your team

Have you ever watched those reality TV shows where they dump people in a house or an island for a couple of months? Apart from the entertainment value (or not as the case may be), it is interesting to watch what happens over time, isn't it? You get to see personalities emerging, conflict arising and people vying for their place in the group. Teams at work are somewhat similar, in the sense that there is a human dynamic involved and this is why the role of the leader is so exciting. Yes, it also makes it quite challenging, but without the people dimension, it would be very boring.

As a leader, you will need to be a good team builder, even if you are taking over an already established team. At the end of the day, your success and that of your team are interdependent, so this is a priority area for you. In this chapter, we will explore a range of issues relevant to developing and sustaining effective teams.

" Your success and that of your team are interdependent. "

Principles of team effectiveness

Before we explore the specific teambuilding activities you must undertake, we will consider the broader topic of team effectiveness, for it is relevant here. You should recognise that teams are dynamic entities in their own right, evolving in either a positive or negative manner, depending on the prevailing circumstances. Some teams grow to a very high level, whereas others struggle to gel from the moment they are created. Understanding the principles of team development is essential, so that you can later use this knowledge to your advantage.

There are various models that describe the stages of team development and they can be helpful in terms of recognising that teams change over time. However, one of the drawbacks with such models is that they are based on the assumption that all members of the team join at the same time and remain together for the lifespan of the team. This may be applicable when thinking of teams established for a particular reason, such as a project team, but the reality will be that the composition of your team will constantly change, due to employee turnover. As such, models that describe various team development stages in a progressive life-cycle can be somewhat misleading for the first-time leader.

A more helpful option is for you to consider differing *states of team effectiveness*. After all, a team is judged on its ability to achieve the required outcomes, not necessarily on how long it has been in existence. There are three states of team effectiveness:

▶ At one end of the scale, a team can be described as being *ineffective*, from the point of view of achieving outcomes. This could be due to the fact that it is new, or it could be because morale is low with lots of conflict, which is making the team underperform.

▶ On the other hand, a team could be *excelling*, whereby it is achieving its outcomes beyond the level of expectation.

▶ In the middle, a team can be described as *effective*, in the sense that it achieves its outcomes to the required standard and is generally working well.

These three states of team performance are described below:

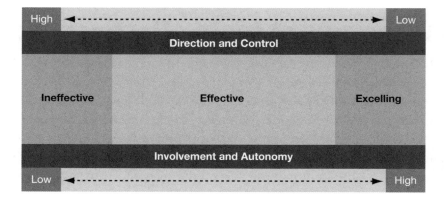

You will quickly notice the linkage between the states of team effectiveness and the three leadership styles discussed earlier, for they are closely related:

▶ Where a team is *ineffective,* it requires the *steering* style of leadership.

▶ An *effective* team responds best to *engaging* styles.

▶ A team that is *excelling* will require the application of the *facilitating* leadership style.

It is important that you again view these three states of team effectiveness as being quite fluid, rather than three separate boxes within which everything fits neatly. One of the advantages of the effectiveness model is that it more closely matches the realities of life at work. Teams can readily float between the three states. For example:

▶ A team could be excelling in achieving outcomes, but if work practices suddenly change, they may become less effective or even ineffective for a short period until they get used to the new system.

▶ A team that was effective might become ineffective for a time, if a number of key team members leave within a short period of time.

Naturally, as a leader, you will want your team to spend as little time as possible in the ineffective state and the goal is to have a team that is excelling. Take a moment to consider past teams you have worked in.

Reflection

Give some thought to a team you have previously worked in or work in now and consider the following:

Team effectiveness

▶ How would you describe that team most of the time: ineffective, effective or excelling?

▶ How could you tell when they were in one state of effectiveness or another?

▶ What did the leader do that caused this?

▶ What could have been done to make the team more effective than it was?

Keep a note of your thoughts for later use.

Building an effective team

There are many factors to be considered when building a team. You should not forget that the quality of your leadership will have a direct impact here, for the more effective the leader, the better the team. So working hard to be a great leader will be your personal contribution to the teambuilding process.

With regard to the other elements to consider, no one thing on its own will lead to the development of a successful team. Rather, it's a combination of eight building-blocks that combine together to make teams work. It will be your responsibility to ensure that each of these components is in place.

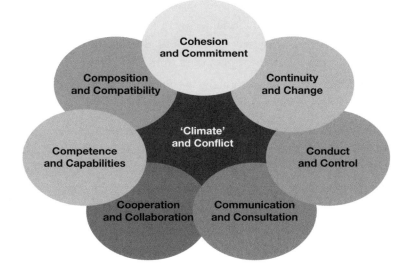

You should also recognise that these key elements of teams are interdependent, so you will need to take a holistic view. In the absence of any of these factors, teamwork is diminished and the potential for conflict increases.

Building-block 1 – cohesion and commitment

Every team needs cohesion and commitment to get them moving in the right direction. Without cohesion, a team lacks purpose and often ends up being a team in name only, comprised in reality of sub-groups or cliques. In order to get cohesion between the different individuals in your team, you will need to define a clear vision and common goals that have real meaning for them. Describing the purpose as being 'to make more money for the company' is unlikely to have any inspirational value for your team.

> **Every team needs cohesion and commitment.**

You will therefore have to bring it down a notch to make it relevant and the challenge will be to identify factors that resonate with them.

Vision

As leader, you will need to develop your own vision for your team because that will give you a clearer picture of what you are hoping to achieve with them. Then you must communicate this in various ways and, where appropriate, involve the team members in defining the overall common purpose. Some people are fearful or embarrassed by such terms as 'vision' as they seem corny or indeed jargony. They might also seem too lofty an idea for you as a first-time leader. Yes, the concept of vision can be, and indeed has been oversold and underdelivered, but that doesn't mean the idea is wrong. Having a clear vision for your team is hugely important and if you are not comfortable with this word, don't use it, but do take the principles on board.

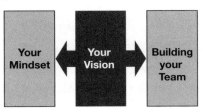

Commitment

To be effective as a unit, you will also need all team members to be committed to the organisation, the team and the agreed common goals. Of course, you cannot force people to be committed, and there are elements here that may be beyond your control. Wider issues, such as how your organisation values its employees, will naturally impact on this; indeed, if general morale across the enterprise is poor, you will have a challenge on your hands to counteract its effects. However, even if this is the case, you need to focus on this issue with your team and build as much loyalty as you can.

Building-block 2 – composition and compatibility

The composition and compatibility of the team have an important role to play in determining its effectiveness. The make-up of your team must be such that there is a diversity of characters and skills available and that there is some degree of rapport between them. Whilst your team members don't have to be best friends, nor must they all act or think alike, there must be synergy.

If you are taking over an existing team, you may not be able to influence composition and compatibility issues in the short term. Where you will have a chance to directly influence it will be in the recruitment of new team members. Consider the following points for the future:

▶ Ensure that you always have direct input into the recruitment of your team members.

▶ Make sure you are trained in interview skills, so you can choose between the best candidates.

▶ Develop and use 'profiles' to ensure that those recruited to the team match your expectations.

▶ Where resources are available, use more scientific profiling tools and psychometric tests as part of recruitment.

Too often, leaders give little thought to this area and new members are brought into the team who do not fit with the overall ethos. This can create significant problems.

Remember, it will always be much harder for you to remove a 'bad egg' once they are in place, than it will be for you to prevent them from joining the team in the first place.

Building-block 3 – competence and capabilities

All team members must have the required competences to undertake the specific tasks allocated to them. Without this, their team mates are expected to compensate for their shortcomings and this will cause friction. As a leader, you must make sure that each individual has the necessary skills to do their work, and you should take an active role in ensuring that everyone has continuous access to formal training and development. However, you can play a more direct role in enhancing competence through the use of coaching and delegation.

Coaching will be an important tool for you as a leader and should be seen as having two dimensions:

Types of Coaching	
Outcome-focused	**People-focused**
▸ Aimed at improving job-related skills ▸ Can be initiated by team members asking for help or guidance ▸ Can arise from you identifying shortcomings in their performance ▸ Focused on making sure that team members can do their job to the required standard	▸ Aimed at personal development of the individual ▸ Mostly used with high potential individuals you wish to help progress ▸ Generally initiated by you ▸ Focuses on broader issues such as personal development and not just on their current job skills

Spending time on either type of coaching and helping individuals to improve will naturally boost work outcomes, but it also shows that you care about them so you should make it one of your priorities.

Another useful developmental tool available to you will be delegation, which you should use to maximum effect. However, there are many misconceptions about the role and function of delegation:

▶ As a leader there will be many tasks that you must *allocate* among team members on a day-to-day basis and this is normal within the sphere of the role.

▶ *Delegation* is somewhat different and relates to tasks that have wider importance, which do not currently form part of an individual's job description.

▶ By delegating important tasks that are part of your remit, you free up your time to concentrate on other critical issues.

▶ For the person you are delegating to, they are taking on a task that is not required of them, but they do so because they see it as an opportunity to grow and develop.

Consequently, delegation should always be seen as having benefits both for you as the leader and for the person to whom you are delegating. It is a win–win situation. Given its nature, not everyone in the team will want to participate. It should mainly be targeted at team members who are keen to develop their skills and knowledge base. The process of delegation requires you to:

▶ Identify the task to delegate

▶ Select the right person to delegate it to

▶ Provide training and guidance

▶ Coach them on an ongoing basis

▶ Follow up the completion of the task.

Remember, you always retain ultimate accountability for that task, but you delegate responsibility to another person to complete it.

Building-block 4 – cooperation and collaboration

It should come as no surprise that to be effective, teams need to work closely together and share the workload evenly. What is perhaps not so obvious is that as a leader, you will be in a position to actively facilitate improved cooperation and collaboration within your team by the manner in which you allocate the workload on an ongoing basis. You should be proactive in how you encourage team members to cooperate and collaborate.

Frequently Asked

Is it a good idea to use team-based approaches to problem-solving?

Once you are established in the role, you should promote team-based approaches to tackle work problems as often as possible. When faced with issues that require significant analysis and exploration, don't be afraid to develop sub-teams to make suggestions as to a range of solutions that could be implemented.

By adopting this approach, you are not losing control, as you will define the parameters within which any solution must fit. Through encouraging collaboration, you not only generate better ideas, but you show that you value and respect your team. Collaboration with your team is a sign of strength, not weakness, and the more you develop your relationship with them, the more effective the collaborative approach becomes.

> **Collaboration with your team is a sign of strength, not weakness.**

Another important consideration here is the danger of cliques forming within your team. This happens all the time and at first there might not seem to be a major problem with this. But it should be of concern to you, because a clique is in effect a team within a team and often they form conflicting goals, which are at variance with the overall cohesion of the team. This is not to say that individuals cannot exercise their right to mix with whom they like, but the formation of cliques is different and can be detrimental to overall team performance. You should proactively tackle such issues as they arise.

Building-block 5 – communication and consultation

Communication and consultation comprise the life-blood of all successful teams and it is through regular, structured and effective communication that common bonds are formed and conflict is addressed before it escalates. As a leader, you must establish appropriate mechanisms to facilitate better communication.

Communication at work tends to be focused upon outcome-related matters and little separate time is devoted to dealing with team concerns. As a leader, you should seek to address this imbalance with your team. This can be relatively easily achieved by holding daily briefings, which have an outcome focus, and monthly team meetings which also have an outcome focus, but allow time to focus on team-related matters. There will of course be other meetings, but introducing these two forms of communication should be your early priority.

Daily briefings

▶ Keep them short, to the point and outcome focused.

▶ Use them to clarify with the team the work requirements for the day.

▶ They are not designed to be two-way discussions, for that would take too long, but of course opportunities are provided to team members to seek clarification on issues relating to the day's work.

▶ They are an opportunity for you to provide direction and to give regular feedback to the team.

Due to the fact that they are short, usually around 10 minutes, many leaders overlook their importance and believe that missing a daily briefing, or not holding them at all, makes no difference.

Frequently Asked

I don't see the need for daily briefings. It's only a couple of minutes: what's the point?

Some leaders use excuses for not conducting daily briefings, ranging from there is no time, or that shift patterns mean everyone would not be there, to the fact that the work is the same every day so there would be nothing to say. But this is a major misconception for a number of reasons.

First, taken in isolation, a 10-minute briefing is really not of great importance, but it is their collective value over a working year that has significance. A 10-minute briefing held five days a week, 50 weeks of the year leads to 2,500 minutes of communication with the team, or in other words over 40 hours per year!

It is this total impact of the direction and feedback provided during the year which makes briefings such a critical tool for the leader. In addition, holding daily briefings also reminds the team, in a subconscious way, that you are the leader and they are a team.

A further advantage of holding briefings is that by bringing the team together on a daily basis, you will be able to gauge the mood and dynamics of the team over time, which will help you to monitor overall team 'climate', which we will discuss later. You will naturally see individuals throughout the day, but this is your chance to view them as a unit, and you will quickly get a sense as to the atmosphere and relationships. So bringing everyone together for a few minutes is vitally important at the start of each day or shift.

Monthly team meetings

To facilitate opportunities to discuss matters relating to team performance in detail, you should formally meet with your team once a month. These meetings should have a set agenda, which is contributed to by your team and circulated in advance. Part of the meeting will deal with work-related matters, but a specific proportion of time should be allocated to discussing team-focused concerns. The importance of these meetings is that they allow the team to explore matters in detail with you, so that problems don't fester and develop into areas of conflict. Such meetings also provide you with an opportunity to offer more detailed feedback on team perform-ance and to constantly reinforce your vision and the common goals. As such, they are critical in helping you to sustain team development.

Building-block 6 – conduct and control

An important element in developing an effective team is how the conduct and behaviour of the team, collectively and individually, are monitored and controlled over time. The concept of conditioning has relevance here too, for if you allow unacceptable conduct or behaviour to persist, then you send out the message that they are acceptable and very soon you will see them more frequently. Consequently, as leader, you will need to watch out for conduct that you feel is inappropriate and deal with it early.

The wider issue of the various personalities and attitudes that you will encounter in your team is also worth discussing here. In any team, you will have team members who broadly fall into three categories:

▶ Those who are mostly *positive* in their attitude and behaviour

▶ Those who are more *negative* in their attitude and behaviour

▶ Those who fall somewhere in between; let's call these the *floaters*, as they can shift back and forth depending upon circumstances.

What percentage of each category you will have in your team is impossible to calculate, for many factors influence it. However, in general it is fair to say that most people fall into either the positive or floating category. Your main focus will therefore have to be on the majority and not the minority. Sadly, this doesn't always happen and too often the negative team members get more focus.

Action

Imagine you are leader of a team of 10, with eight being generally positive or floaters and two being consistently negative. Who will get most of your attention? We should say the eight, but the reverse is often true and there are in fact many hidden rewards for being negative. First, negative characters tend to be more vociferous and demanding and take up more of your time. So, in effect, the first reward for being negative is getting more attention. Second, when there is extra work to be done or when you need something above and beyond the norm, who are you more likely to approach? Yes, the positive or floating team members for obvious reasons. Therefore, the second reward for being negative is getting less work. Nobody intends this to happen, but it does.

A simple example of how negative individuals end up getting more attention which you will have likely seen many times already is what often occurs at the team meetings mentioned earlier. Often at such meetings, the negative individuals are allowed to dominate and everyone in the team has to sit and listen to the minority view.

This is bad practice in action. You should always ensure that the negatives are not allowed to dominate. For if you do, you will find their numbers increasing, as often some floaters will join the bandwagon. Consequently, you must recognise and reward positive behaviour and your primary focus should always be on the positives and floaters. Of course, you must deal with the difficult individuals, but

> *" You must recognise and reward positive behaviours. "*

you must not allow them to monopolise your thinking or your time.

If the positive employees feel valued, then by their nature they will continue to support you with increased effort and the floaters will see the rewards in being positive. Eventually, in this environment, the negatives feel isolated and either come onside over time or are squeezed out. Of course, all of this has to be subtly achieved and again you can see the importance for you in having the ability to control your own reactions and communicate effectively.

Building-block 7 – continuity and change

These elements are obviously polar opposites, but they need to be considered in unison. All teams require some degree of continuity, because too much change can be daunting for most people. However, as leader you shouldn't allow ruts to set in, whereby change is avoided simply because it can be challenging to handle. Sometimes at work we continue to do things 'because they have always been done this way' and you must challenge inertia where it is within your control to make changes for the better. On the other hand, change just for the sake of it can be counterproductive and really annoys team members, so any changes should lead to improvement of some kind.

We will look at some of the practicalities of dealing with change in the following chapter.

Building-block 8 – climate and conflict

The overall 'climate' or atmosphere within your team will be a direct outcome of the other building-blocks being in place. Team spirit and motivation are so important that you will have to watch closely how your team interact with one another.

You will not be able to influence the levels of climate and conflict of the team in the short run, but you will need to put in place the relevant measures in the other building-blocks which will cumulatively impact on overall team climate. Keep in mind:

▶ There will be highs and lows, but if you start to see prolonged periods when people are unhappy, then you will need to take the necessary steps to deal with the problem.

▶ Through your actions in other areas, you are aiming to create an environment in your team where conflict is not so prevalent.

▶ Conflict will still happen and when it does you will have to address it quickly so that it doesn't get out of hand.

We will also be dealing with issues such as motivation and conflict in the following chapter.

There is no step-by-step path to follow in building a team, as the range of activities is broad and not necessarily to be followed in a particular sequence. The eight building-blocks will give you a focus for what should be done. You will recognise that, if you are taking over an existing team, many elements within the eight blocks may already be in place to some degree and your target will be to maximise their impact. If you are setting up a team for the first time, then the workload will obviously be greater. For the moment, concentrate on getting a general picture of what needs to be done and we will return later to this area with further guidance on how to build your team.

As a conclusion to this chapter, consider some of the teams you have previously worked in and reflect on the following points.

Action
Give some thought again to a team you have previously worked in or currently work in and consider the following:

Team building-blocks
Taking each of the eight building-blocks, consider how well your past team(s) performed in relation to the following:

▶ Were there good levels of *cohesion and commitment* within the team? If not, why not?

▶ Did the *composition and compatibility* of the team help its effectiveness? If not, why not?

▶ Did individuals within the team have the necessary *competence* and did the team overall have the right *capabilities* to be an effective one?

If not, was anything done about it?

▶ What were the levels of *cooperation and collaboration* like? Were they good? If not, how did it feel to work in that team?

▶ Was there good *communication and consultation* within the team? Did you and the other team members feel involved? If not, did that affect how you worked together?

▶ How did the leader of that team maintain the right levels of *conduct and control*? Were they fair? Was everyone clear on what they could and couldn't get away with?

▶ Was there some *continuity* or was there frequent *change*? How was the change handled?

▶ How was the overall *climate and conflict*? Was it an enjoyable team to work in?

Keep a note of your thoughts for later use.

To further guide your thinking in relation to teambuilding, in Part 6 we will examine specific measures you can take within each building-block as you seek to build your team.

As you get ready to lead, you must:	
Stop	**Start**
Focusing on *stages of team development*	Concentrating on the three *states of team effectiveness*
Believing that effective teams just happen	Recognising that teams need to be developed and nurtured
Thinking there is nothing you can do about teambuilding until you start as a leader	Watching teams at work to learn why some teams perform better than others

CHAPTER EIGHT

Common teambuilding concerns

When you ask first-time leaders what are their greatest concerns in relation to teambuilding, which issues do you think come up most frequently? What are your own concerns in this regard? Most likely, you will be worrying about the things that might go wrong, such as conflict or difficult team members causing problems. All first-timers have the same fears and some get quite stressed at the prospect of what could happen. Teams never run completely smoothly, so you should expect some ups and downs, but rest assured there will be more good times than bad.

To help you to prepare for likely challenges, our focus here will be to explore some common problems that arise:

- ▶ Motivating your team
- ▶ Handling conflict
- ▶ Coping with change
- ▶ Dealing with difficult team members.

Like all human resource issues, there is no magic wand, but there are some general principles that will help you. As you read ahead, try again to apply the content here to your existing team, or to those that you have worked with in the past.

Motivating your team

⬥In motivating people, you've got to engage their minds and their hearts. It is good busines to have an employee feel part of the

> entire effort ... I motivate people, I hope, by example – and perhaps by excitement, by having provocative ideas to make others feel involved. *

Rupert Murdoch
Business Leader

Motivating people is never easy and all leaders struggle with this issue to some extent. Sadly, the difficulties associated with motivating your team and the individuals within it never disappear, but it will become easier for you over time.

The first thing to recognise is that there is no one thing that will motivate all the team, all of the time. People are different, so they will not be motivated in the same way, or to the same degree. There are common motivating factors of course, and we have already covered many of them throughout this book. Your team members are more likely to be motivated by an effective leader, when communication is open and regular, when they feel valued and when their achievements are recognised and appreciated.

Motivating your team will be primarily about two challenges:

- ▶ Creating a 'total environment', which contains as many of the common motivators as possible.
- ▶ Getting to know your team members as individuals, so that you can identify their individual motivators.

There are many established theories regarding motivation, in life and at work, but as we have done in all areas, we will try to avoid an overly theoretical analysis of the subject and instead concentrate on how you can motivate in practice.

If you ask a group of employees what motivates them, frequently the first answer they give is money: 'Give me more money and I'll be more motivated'. Whilst this is often the initial reply, when analysed further, money is actually not so much a motivator but more a factor that makes people feel happy or unhappy. Don't get it wrong, money is a crucial factor in the work environment, as we don't get out of bed each day solely for the love of it. We do so because we need money.

« Give me more money and I'll be more motivated. »

Frequently Asked

People are really only motivated by money, aren't they?

Money is an important component, but as a motivator it has at best short-term positive impacts. For example, if your current boss was able to give you and each of your team members a large increase in your next pay-cheque, do you think you would be happy? Well of course you would. But would you be more motivated? Perhaps, in the short term. But after a few weeks you would have assimilated the extra income into your lifestyles and would be looking for the next increase.

To use money as a motivator, you would have to continuously increase the rate of pay and this is not sustainable in the longer term. In any case there is no guarantee this would lead to higher levels of motivation. Also, this is one area over which you as a first-time leader will have no influence.

The important thing to remember here is that money is at the root of why we work, but it does not motivate us over the long term. Where money can become a motivating factor is when it is linked to improved performance and many industries have various financial packages designed to motivate. But the establishment and operation of such schemes will also be beyond your control as a first-time leader, so it is better to focus on areas where you can more directly influence motivation levels.

Research and experience have shown that there are other things that serve as motivators for people and in no order of importance, these include:

- ▶ Positive relationships with their boss
- ▶ Feeling valued and respected
- ▶ Knowing what the company is trying to achieve
- ▶ Good two-way communication
- ▶ Positive team spirit
- ▶ Opportunities for learning new things
- ▶ Possibilities for career advancement

▶ Regular feedback on the performance

▶ Being acknowledged for work well done

▶ Variety in the day-to-day work

▶ Job security.

Obviously not everyone is motivated by the same things on this list. As a leader, you will have to ensure that as many of these motivators are in place as possible. By knowing your team as individuals, you can then focus on addressing their specific motivators.

Work should be enjoyable as well as challenging, and team members should feel that they benefit from their interactions with one another. You should also encourage a social dimension to the team and periodically organise events where the team can interact outside the work environment, beyond the pub. This is particularly true when the team has achieved something of significance.

Action

Give some thought now to the area of motivation and consider the following points:

▶ On a blank sheet of paper list the five things that motivate you most at work.

▶ Now select 10 friends or work colleagues and ask them for their top five.

▶ Compare the lists and you will find fairly similar responses.

▶ Consider how you might use this information when you become a leader.

Keep a note of your thoughts for later use.

Handling conflict

Conflict is a natural feature of human interactions. In any group, there will always be factors that arise which lead to conflict, such as clashes of personality, differences of opinions, or contrasting beliefs and values. In particular, the workplace with its time pressures, deadlines and range of personalities is the perfect breeding-ground for conflict. The levels of conflict you will experience in your team will depend greatly upon how well you address the issues highlighted in the team building-blocks described previously.

However, no matter how well you build your team, conflict will still occur from time to time, so you will have to deal with it. It is important to recognise that although resolving conflict is difficult, you should not avoid it, for then it will simply fester and worsen. Conflict rarely dissipates without proactive action being taken by the leader. There are so many forms of conflict that can arise that it is impossible to address all possibilities here, so we will concentrate on conflict from two perspectives:

> **❝Although resolving conflict is difficult, you should not avoid it.❞**

1   When you are directly in conflict with another person or persons

2   When conflict occurs between individuals in your team.

When considering conflict that involves you directly, the first point is to examine your own reactions to it. It should be clear that aggressive or passive behaviours will not help you in such situations. When you lose control, you are no longer capable of being rational as your emotions take over. As a rule, the greater the *emotional* element, the lower the *rational* element, for they always move in opposite directions. So, your first concern in conflict resolution should be to take on board what we have already said about controlling your emotions and reactions.

> **❝The greater the emotional element, the lower the rational *element*.❞**

In addition, you must address the emotional aspect of the individual with whom you are in conflict. You need to make it clear that you will discuss and listen to what they have to say, but you will not accept their overuse of emotion. Then it is a matter of defining the real issue and once the problem is clear, moving towards solving it. Constant arguing over an already identified problem is unproductive, so you will need to shift it to how things can be improved. This all sounds so simple doesn't it? You know it won't be, but if you can be calm and firm, then you are well on your way to resolving conflict that directly involves you.

Now to the wider issue of conflict between different individuals in your team, which may or may not involve you. In developing your ability to deal with this type of conflict, it is important to accept that not all conflict is bad. Conflict can be:

▶ *Constructive* when it leads to better ideas, or

▶ *Destructive* when it damages relationships which are then carried into other aspects of work.

Constructive conflict

Heated debate, reasoned argument and other such forms of conflict – when focused on issues, not personalities – should be encouraged not stifled. Passion, which is a positive force, can bring people into conflict, but killing the conflict prematurely can also destroy some of the passion. Your role as a leader in such circumstances will be to ensure that the heat in the situation is not allowed to boil over and that the parties focus on the issue at hand. You may end up taking a direct role in defining the solution, depending upon how the matter develops, but you should initially play a facilitation role to see whether the parties can resolve it themselves. The key with handling constructive conflict will be for you to control and guide the direction it takes.

Destructive conflict

A more difficult challenge will be to deal with the different forms of destructive conflict that arise, the nature of which will be varied. In general terms, destructive conflict occurs where it is adding no value in either the short or long term. In other words, it's not leading to better outcomes, improved relationships or enhanced efficiency. Such conflict can often take the form of personality clashes and your role here will be to take direct action to resolve it. Some points you will need to consider when dealing with destructive conflict:

▶ The starting point is to draw a line in the sand by letting the parties involved know that you are aware of it and are not prepared to accept it.

▶ Your next step will be to attempt to play a mediation role in trying to define the issues at hand and to get them to agree on a resolution.

▶ This will often require you to meet individually with those involved and then bringing them together to agree a way forward.

▶ You could just tell them to stop, as is often done, but don't think that this resolves the conflict, it simply buries it. It will continue, but will just be hidden from you.

In many cases, you will not be able to reach a suitable resolution – particularly if it is a matter of two individuals simply disliking each other. When this happens, you must impose the required result. You cannot get them to like each other, but you can define the behaviour that you are prepared to accept from them. Then you must monitor compliance with what you have imposed. Failure to comply should have consequences, as you must send out a consistently strong message that you will not accept destructive conflict within the team.

Action

In the coming days and weeks, start to pay particular attention to conflict situations you see arising at work. As you do, think about:

▶ Is this constructive or destructive conflict?

▶ What are the reactions of those involved?

▶ Is there lots of emotion with little rationality?

▶ Are they focused on real issues or arguing about irrelevancies?

▶ Who is trying to resolve it?

▶ How was it resolved?

▶ If it is not resolved, is it having wider effects within the team?

▶ What can you learn from it to help you in future as a leader?

Keep a note of your thoughts for later use.

Coping with change

Change is a fact of life in any business today and, as a leader, you will have to be comfortable in dealing with it. In terms of handling change, as a general rule, the more involvement people have in determining the nature and direction of changes affecting them, the more easily they will buy into and support the implementation process. The reverse is also true of course and the more powerless they feel, the more resistance you will see. This is not so hard to figure out, but the reality of work is that not all changes can be implemented through consultation. There are many aspects to change and again it is not feasible to address them all here but rather to give you a general sense of what to look out for.

You must become an enthusiastic promoter of change, not for the sake of it, but when it brings about better results. But don't expect everyone else to feel the same, because you will invariably encounter quite a few negative reactions.

Frequently Asked

Some people can never cope with change; how should I deal with them?

Most people are willing to grasp change readily, depending upon how it is presented and handled. However, there are others who fear it and fight it as much as they can. The important point for you to recognise is that there is a human dimension to handling change which has to be addressed at some stage during the process. Better to try to deal with discontent or fear at the outset, than to ignore the natural human reactions and deal with rebellion at a later stage. Of course, there are those who instinctively resist change but the majority of people often have valid concerns surrounding change.

So when you hear things like 'that'll never work here', don't immediately see this as the negative sign it appears to be at face value. What it often means is 'convince me' and helping your team to cope with change will often require a selling process on your behalf, particularly in an environment where there have been a lot of ineffective changes made in the past.

Remember, you cannot move people from fear of change to commitment in one single step and your initial goal should always be just to get people to try it. If it is for the better, then they will see the benefits and resistance will diminish over time.

The context for change

How you handle change affecting your team will depend upon how much control you have over it. As a first-time leader, you will not always have a say about changes that affect your area, as decisions will often be driven from a more senior level. When this arises, you should at least try to influence the nature of the decisions that are made above you, if you think they will have a detrimental effect on your team. You must also recognise that your power to do so will be limited, but your role is always to represent your team's interests as best you can.

Sometimes you will simply have to live with an unpopular decision and it will be your job to make the necessary changes happen within your team. This can be difficult for you, but as mentioned earlier, you must never let your team feel that you disagree with the decision, even if you do. If they see that you are not behind it, then they will resist its implementation more fervently. Your role in such circumstances will be to make the best of a bad lot and to project a positive image for the team, supporting them with implementing the change. You may have to let them offload on you until they come to terms with it, but that will sometimes be your role as leader – to take the flak.

> **That will sometimes be your role as leader – to take the flak.**

When you do have direct control over the change in question, you should seek to apply different approaches depending upon the situation. In effect you will use different leadership styles in handling change. Sometimes you will feel that certain changes are required, which your team members might not agree with. Your task will not be to try to force the change through, but you should be prepared to meet with the team to explain your rationale. You may not be willing to reverse your decision, but you are happy to listen to their concerns. In effect you are adopting a *low steering style* of leadership here. On other occasions you may want to give the team greater input into the final nature of the change and you will allow them to make suggestions within certain parameters, which is in effect the *engaging style* of leadership. So, the approach you take to deal with change will depend upon its context.

Some general points to consider in relation to handling change:

- ▶ Change must lead to tangible benefits, if your team are expected to buy into it.
- ▶ You will often have to 'sell' the change to your team members.
- ▶ Change just for the sake of it winds people up and should be avoided.
- ▶ The more input that your team have into the change process, the less negativity and resistance you will generally encounter.
- ▶ Include your team members in decision-making around change, where possible.
- ▶ The bigger the change, the more difficult it can be for people and you need to take a strong leadership role in making the changes happen.
- ▶ The implementation of change should be time bound, for continuous change can be disheartening.
- ▶ Make sure that you define clear implementation plans and that you adhere to deadlines.
- ▶ Show benefits as early as possible in the change process, so people see the value of it.
- ▶ Offer lots of support and guidance as people seek to work through the change.
- ▶ Change processes provide ideal opportunities for the negative team members to 'stir things up'. Pay particular attention to the influence they are exerting at such times.

Action

Think of a recent change that took place in your workplace and consider the following points (try to pick something relatively major):

- ▶ How was the change handled? Was there good communication before, during and after?
- ▶ Did people feel they had some input, or was it forced through?
- ▶ In either case, how did the people affected by the change react?

> ▶ Who was leading the change?
>
> ▶ Did they play a positive role in helping to implement it?
>
> ▶ What might you learn from this example to help you as a leader in future?
>
> Keep a note of your thoughts for later use.

Dealing with difficult team members

It is very important that you recognise the damage that a difficult, uncommitted or disillusioned team member can do to overall team effectiveness. They will act as a weight that holds everyone down and rarely will they play a passive role within the team. Often they will seek to influence the thinking of others and undermine your position as leader; therefore you will have to deal with their effects sooner or later. Better if it is sooner, before they have a chance to spread dissent. Unacceptable behaviour of all kinds and worse still negativity are like viruses and will spread to others if you don't address them quickly.

When faced with a team member who is behaving unacceptably, your first concern is to ensure that this is not translated into poor quality in their work and then, as mentioned, that they are not playing games within the team. It goes without saying that all such matters should be dealt with on a one-to-one basis. You should begin by spending time trying to win them around, but this may be wishful thinking in a lot of cases. However, you still need to try and with the right approach it can be done. What you will have to highlight for them is that you are happy to try to deal with anything within your control that may be affecting their performance, but that you are not prepared to accept their disruptive behaviour.

This will require some subtlety on your behalf (and is another example of why you will need the right qualities and skills to succeed as a leader) because rarely will they openly admit that there is anything wrong with their behaviour. In fact, they will usually deny it and often try to project the problem back at you by accusing you of picking on them. But see this for what it is and stick with it. You may need to monitor their performance over a period to identify specific examples where the problematic behaviour is evident.

Remember, you are not singling them out, as you will be monitoring the performance of all your team, but you are approaching them differently in terms of leadership style, because they are acting in an unacceptable manner. It is critical that you spend time at the beginning getting the individual in question to recognise that there is a problem, or failing that, making it clear to them what your concerns are. It is important to understand that an individual will rarely make an effort to improve; if they don't accept that they have a problem in the first place.

Where this will end up in the long term depends upon the individual in question and how they respond to your approaches. The result you get will also be affected by the skills you display in dealing with it. Further points to keep in mind when dealing with such individuals:

- On first raising the issue with them, you must make it clear that there is a problem and you will no longer accept it.
- You begin by being prepared to discuss the issue with them, but only if they accept there is a problem.
- If they respond to your approach and perform to the required standard and do not seek to cause disgruntlement within the team, then they are having a benign effect and you will have to just live with it.
- If their work deteriorates, or if they continue sowing seeds of discontent, then you must not ignore it.
- On subsequent occasions in dealing with this person, you would focus on their progress or lack of it, since you first spoke to them. You will become more and more prescriptive in what you expect from them if they fail to respond to your efforts.
- In essence, you will shift from an engaging style of leadership, to one of steering.

If they fail to come onside over time, then you need to start thinking of how they can be eased from the team, in line with company policy and appropriate legal requirements. But that is why there is a disciplinary process. However, only use it after you have tried other approaches, because once you do, there is rarely a way back.

As a conclusion to this chapter, complete the following exercise.

Action

Think of difficult or disruptive individuals in your team. In the coming weeks, try to watch from a distance how your team leader deals with them:

▶ Does the leader deal with the issue or ignore it?

▶ Does the leader challenge the individuals publicly or in private?

▶ Does their approach work?

▶ If not, what happens to the individuals in question?

Keep a note of your thoughts for later use.

You are likely to face some or all of these common concerns early in your career as a leader and should prepare for them by watching how such matters are handled within your team. There are no quick-fix solutions to any of them, but if you understand the principles described here, you will be on the right track.

As you get ready to lead, you must:	
Stop	**Start**
Viewing money as a motivator	Recognising that no one thing will motivate everyone to the same degree
Believing that all negative reactions to change are bad	Understanding the human dynamic associated with change
Thinking that all conflict is bad	Differentiating between constructive and destructive conflict and learn how to deal with each
Wishing there was a magic formula for dealing with difficult team members	Developing your skills so that you can deal with such individuals effectively

Reflect upon

Working with teams is what makes the leader's role so interesting. It is also what makes it so challenging. In relation to the teambuilding issues covered here, watch and learn from good and bad practice in action every day in your organisation. This will help you to prepare for leadership. As you do so, keep the following key messages with you:

▶ Successful teams do not just happen, they must be built and sustained. A combination of eight building-blocks must be considered.

▶ Teams are not static, they shift between different states of effectiveness.

▶ People at work are more likely to be motivated when communication is open and regular, when they feel valued, and when their achievements are recognised and appreciated.

▶ Motivating your team at work is primarily about creating a 'total environment' which contains as many common motivators as possible.

▶ You must also get to know your team as individuals so that you can identify their personal motivators.

▶ Conflict is a reality in any group or team. Although dealing with conflict may be difficult, you must take proactive steps to address it. Ignoring destructive conflict is a bad idea.

▶ Change is an important feature of leadership and you should promote change, when it is for the best and not just for the sake of it.

▶ Each change situation has to be handled differently and the amount of control you have over the change will determine how you deal with it.

▶ As a general rule, try to involve your team in decision-making around change and when you cannot do this, at least be willing to address their areas of concern as best you can.

▶ Do not allow repetitive and unacceptable behaviour by individuals within the team to go unchallenged.

In Part 5 we will shift the focus to summarising what you have learned about yourself so far and translating that into concrete action to help you to get ready to lead.

Setting Personal Goals

Are you ready to lead?

> 'Before you are a leader, success is all about growing yourself.
> When you become a leader, success is all about growing others.'
>
> Jack Welch
> Former Chairman and CEO of General Electric

The previous chapters have given you plenty of food for thought about your current potential to lead and don't be alarmed if you feel you have many gaps to bridge. This is not unusual and just be thankful that you have identified your areas for improvement at an early stage. Many don't, until it's too late. Others fool themselves into thinking they are further ahead than they really are. A long list simply means you have made a detailed and honest evaluation of yourself.

If you want to be truly ready to lead, then you must grow and develop in preparation, by addressing the areas for improvement that relate to how you think and act as a leader. This is a learning process that will take time and you must start by setting personal goals to focus your efforts.

In Part 5 you will find answers to important questions such as:

▶ How can I set personal goals?
▶ What personal improvement goals do I need?

To guide you, five personal goals are also defined which represent the common development needs of those seeking to make the step up into leadership.

CHAPTER NINE

Setting personal goals

How many New Year's resolutions did you make this year? Can you even remember them? How many did you stick with? If you are the same as everyone else, they probably went out the window by the end of January. We all have a tendency to let things slide over time, but in your quest for leadership you must not let that happen. You will not become a great leader just by hoping for the best – you have to be proactive by setting and achieving goals based on turning your current weaknesses into strengths. In this chapter, we will explore an easy-to-use framework to help you to set and achieve goals.

The goal achievement framework

❝My biggest motivation? Just to keep challenging myself, I see life almost like one long university education that I never had – every day I'm learning something new.❞

Richard Branson
Business Leader

Leaders, at any level, are results orientated and you must be too if you want to make it. If you don't, you drift and you definitely want to avoid going nowhere. To assist you, we will consider a general approach to defining and working towards your goals. This will help you both in the

❝ *You definitely want to avoid going nowhere.* ❞

context of your own personal development, but it will also be useful for any work-related objectives you will establish in future.

Achieving your goals obviously requires you to define them in the first place and then demands that you are both *efficient* and *effective* in moving towards them. Efficiency and effectiveness are not the same thing. Efficiency comes from having some approach to planning, such as a diary, which you adhere to daily. Using such tools provides structure to your day and allows you to prioritise activities on an ongoing basis.

Being efficient is only part of the equation, as you can actually be efficient without ever achieving your goals. For example, you could be a very organised person at work but that doesn't necessarily mean you are heading in the right direction, it just means you get through the workload at hand efficiently. To be really effective:

▶ You first need to clearly define goals.

▶ Then you must work back from them by identifying the range of activities and tasks that will move you towards those goals.

▶ These activities and tasks must then be scheduled using your planning tools.

▶ You must review progress regularly.

An ability to combine efficiency and effectiveness will turn you into an achiever over the long term. Here is a basic goal achievement framework for you to follow.

Goal Achievement Framework		
Step 1 – Define your *goal*	→	Begin by defining your ***goal*** as clearly as possible. Be as specific as you can and make notes about the end results you want. In other words, paint mental pictures of your goal.
Step 2 – Identify the key *activities*	→	List the key ***activities*** that would be required to achieve this goal. Don't worry at this stage about when these will be done – just try to think of the broad activities that must happen to make this goal a reality. *Brainstorming* is a good tool to use here.
Step 3 – Break these activities into more specific *tasks*.	→	Break these broader activities into more specific ***tasks*** that need to be carried out within that activity.

Goal Achievement Framework		
Step 4 – Think also about the *sequencing* of these tasks.	→	Do certain tasks need to be carried out before others? Put the tasks into a logical **sequence**. This will help with deciding deadlines etc.
Step 5 – Develop *timelines* for each task	→	For each of the tasks that you identify, define **timelines** for when you would like to implement them with a clear finish date. Depending on the goal in question, timelines might be quite specific or could be structured on a short, medium or long-term basis.
Step 6 – Use a *scheduling tool* to keep you on track	→	Use your existing **scheduling tool** to plan these tasks, including start and finish dates as appropriate.
Step 7 – *Monitor progress* at regular intervals	→	**Monitor progress** at frequent intervals so that any drift can be identified early.

This framework provides you with an easy-to-follow mechanism for working towards your goals. Here is an example of this approach in action:

Step 1

Imagine you decided that one of your goals for your team was to achieve high levels of openness and honesty (goal). For illustration purposes, we will say it's now the month of June and you want the measures to help you to achieve this goal to be in place by the end of August.

Step 2

Attaining this goal might involve the following:

1 Increase the levels of communication
2 Host a teambuilding event
3 Hold regular team social events.

Step 3

Within each of these activities a number of tasks would then be required to make it a reality, as set out below.

Activities			
	1. Increase levels of communication	**2. Host teambuilding event**	**3. Hold regular team social events**
Tasks	▸ Introduce daily team briefings ▸ Gather suggestions from team for other communication activities ▸ Introduce a monthly team meeting ▸ Evaluate suggestions and implement most feasible alternatives	▸ Agree aims, format, logistics, etc. ▸ Source suitable external consultants ▸ Get approval and budget from HR Department ▸ Run teambuilding event	▸ Gather suggestions from team as to suitable events ▸ Agree team Social Committee ▸ Define budget and agree how events will be funded ▸ Prepare a schedule of monthly events for first six months

Step 4

You must then put the tasks within each activity into some logical sequence. For example, when considering holding a teambuilding event, the first thing required would be to check what budget would be available (*sequencing*).

Step 5

You need to decide the timeframe for the completion of each of the relevant tasks (*timelines*).

Step 6

Transfer this information to your diary, so you can keep track of progress (*scheduling tool*).

Step 7

You must then review how you are getting on at regular intervals (*monitor progress*).

Based on this example, you could use a goal-setting template something like this:

Step 1- Describe your Goal	To achieve high levels of openness and honesty within the team and to improve team spirit and overall team effectiveness.	
Step 2 - Key Activities	**Steps 3 & 4 - Specific Tasks & Sequencing**	**Step 5 - Timelines**
Now list the general activities that will be required to achieve this goal in this column	*Now break these broader activities into more specific tasks. As you do this, try where possible to sequence the tasks in the order they need to be completed*	*Define timelines when you wish to implement each task. If you do not as yet have specific dates; at least decide if it has a short, medium or long-term focus*
1. Increase levels of communication	Introduce daily team briefings	From 1 June
	Introduce a monthly team meeting	First meeting to be held in last week of June
	Gather suggestions from team for other communication activities	By end 2nd week of June
	Evaluate suggestions and implement most feasible alternatives	By end June
2. Host Teambuilding Event	Get approval and budget from HR Department	By end June
	Source suitable external consultants	By 2nd week in July
	Agree aims, format, logistics etc.	By end July
	Run teambuilding event	Agree date for mid August
3. Hold Regular Team Social Events	Agree team Social Committee	By end 2nd week of June
	Gather suggestions from team as to suitable events	By end June
	Define budget and agree how events will be funded	By mid July
	Schedule a monthly event for the first six months	First event for end of August

Step 6 - On an ongoing basis you must ensure that these tasks actually happen. Use your diary or other scheduling tool

Step 7 – Your scheduling tool will also help you to monitor progress and to check whether you have met your defined deadlines

This is just one example of how the goal achievement framework can be applied in practice, but it should give you a general idea as to how to use it. It is simple to set goals, but not so easy to take the necessary action to realise them, and this approach counteracts this shortcoming. Remember, your daily life at work will be filled with things that need to be done, but not always with tasks that move you towards your goals.

The framework also combines efficiency and effectiveness. You become more *effective*, as you start thinking first about your goals and are consciously moving towards them. You become more *efficient*, because you define the key activities and tasks that need to happen to reach your goals and enter them into your planning system to ensure they happen. This will be a useful approach for you to follow when thinking of the personal goals identified in the next chapter.

As a conclusion to this chapter, complete the following exercise.

Action

Think of a goal you would like to achieve. For this exercise pick any goal – it doesn't have to be related to work.

▶ Work through the seven steps of the goal achievement framework.

▶ Prepare a goal achievement template similar to the example provided in this chapter.

As you get ready to lead, you must:	
Stop	**Start**
Hoping that self-improvement will just happen	Taking proactive steps to make your goals a reality
Thinking that being efficient will be enough	Recognising that you need to be effective as well
Taking an ad hoc approach to achieving your goals	Using the goal achievement framework

10 CHAPTER TEN
The five goals

As you seek to enhance your leadership potential, it is difficult to know where to start, isn't it? You will have lots of development needs, so it may seem a little overwhelming at this point. To give you a head start, five common personal goals for first-time leaders are presented here, which relate to many of the content areas covered so far. You will of course have additional goals you wish to pursue in your quest to develop your capabilities, but these five will give you some focus to begin with:

Goal 1 – Translate your leadership mindset into action

Goal 2 – Strengthen your leadership profile

Goal 3 – Develop your core leadership skills

Goal 4 – Establish networks and mentors

Goal 5 – Change, but stay true to yourself.

For each goal, summary advice is provided and you should use the goal achievement framework to define how you will move towards that goal. Once you have addressed these five goals, you should then define additional goals and develop your action plans from there.

Goal 1 – Translate your leadership mindset into action

The importance of the leader's mindset is well established. Now you need to consider how you will translate your way of thinking into practical steps to follow when you take over your team. Before you start in the role, you will need to have your vision defined as well as the steps you will take to communicate it to them.

Your vision should:

▶ Translate your ultimate goal for your team into more concrete terms.

▶ Describe how you want your team to develop in the ideal world.

▶ Focus on issues such as: how your team will interact with each other, what the acceptable behaviour within the team will be, and what the relationship between you and them will be like.

▶ Give you a starting point by painting a picture of what you would like to achieve with your team.

Simply having a vision doesn't guarantee that you will achieve it of course, but it begins the process. Without this vision in mind, you could end up anywhere in terms of how effective your team becomes. Once you have clarified your vision, you then have to implement a range of measures once you start as a leader to make it a reality. We have discussed many of these in earlier chapters.

Understandably, communicating your vision might be a daunting prospect and it does take some courage to sit the team down and discuss such issues. That is why some managers avoid it, because they lack the confidence to face the challenge. Leaders never ignore this vital move and that is one reason why you have to be an effective communicator to succeed. If you don't transmit your hopes for the team, then they are in effect still thinking in terms of the previous leader's vision and they have no idea of what *your* expectations are. You need to give them this overview of what you hope to achieve as a starting point to getting cohesion and commitment within the team. By not doing this, you allow the negative team members to exercise greater control over the others because, rest assured, they will be transmitting their opinions about you.

Spend time now defining your vision and the actions/tasks that will be required to achieve it.

> **Action**
> Start thinking about your vision for your team and put it into words. Using the goal achievement framework, begin identifying the activities and tasks you will implement when you start as a leader to move you in the right direction.

Goal 2 – Strengthen your leadership profile

❝The quality of a leader is reflected in the standards they set for themselves. ❞

Ray Kroc
Founder of McDonald's

You already know that leaders personify excellence in everything they do and that they are the living embodiment of their vision. You also understand the importance of having a strong leadership profile to support you in the role and should have identified your areas for improvement against the attracting and bridging qualities. Now, you must set about defining how you will strengthen your leadership profile.

One of the most important qualities identified was self-control and you should give this area your particular attention. If you want to be a role model, you need to be in control because effective leaders are never predominantly aggressive or passive. Some important points for you to consider when addressing your self-control:

❝To be a role model, you need to be in control. ❞

▶ First identify whether you have a predisposition towards aggression or passivity.

▶ Isolate the different triggers that bring out this behaviour in you.

▶ Defining your triggers is critical, as it is your responses to these triggers that you proactively need to address.

▶ Sometimes your triggers are not so easily defined, but you have to try to isolate what brings out the negative response in you if you are going to tackle the right issue.

In terms of changing there is no easy answer, despite what certain self-help books might say. You have to try to break the hold that a lifetime of conditioning has over you. If you fail to conquer these problems, then you will 'condition' those around you that these are your predictable behaviour patterns, which gives them even more power over you. In other words, they will learn what your buttons are and they will push them as often as they can. In the end, you will become a sort of interactive video game for them – let's push this button and see what happens!

You should also look at other leadership qualities and select those which you want to really work on.

Action

Start thinking about strengthening your leadership profile. Review each of the leadership qualities discussed earlier and if you haven't already done so, identify your current strengths and areas for improvement. Then pick those qualities you particularly wish to work on, paying special attention to the issue of self-control. For each quality you choose, follow the goal-setting framework and identify practical measures you can take to address your weak areas.

Goal 3 – Develop your core leadership skills

You also need to work on developing your core leadership skills. Some of these, such as your leadership style, won't come into play until you start in the role, but you can watch other leaders in action now and learn from the good and bad practice you witness.

However, you can immediately start to work on improving your ability to communicate. To develop your communication skills you naturally need to consider both content and context.

Some points to remember about *content:*

▶ Thinking before talking will help.
▶ Always plan what you wish to achieve from each communication.

▶ The more important the interaction, the greater the need to plan.

▶ Think of your audience and focus on what you have to say.

▶ Avoid jargon, be yourself.

▶ Clarity and brevity are critical when transmitting your message.

Some points to remember about *context*:

▶ Context relates to tone and body language.

▶ It is influenced by your emotions and self-control.

▶ This will be harder to change.

▶ A useful tool is to see yourself in action. Video yourself when you are making a presentation, as you will get some impression of how you use body language.

▶ Talk to others whom you know and trust, and ask them to give you feedback.

▶ Attend training courses that focus on this area.

As you are developing your ability to communicate, don't forget what we said about becoming a better listener. Start using active listening techniques now.

Action

Give a lot of thought to how you currently communicate, using the results from previous exercises to help you. Pick the most critical areas for improvement and apply the goal-setting framework so that you can define specific tasks you must undertake to improve.

Goal 4 – Establish networks and mentors

This goal is designed to help you as you seek to achieve the first three goals. We said earlier that leaders are born and made. We should probably add something to that. Leaders are born, made and *supported*. You will not be able to make it as a leader all on your own and this is where networks and mentors will be helpful.

Establish networks

Networking is an important concept in work life and, as a first-time leader, it will play a useful role in your development and progression. There are a number of networks to consider:

▶ *Internal networks* – Identify key people within your organisation who will have a significant role in your work life, not just now but in the future, and forge relationships with them over time.

▶ *External networks* – There are many business associations each targeting a specific field and you should be a member of the most important bodies. You should also search for networks where other first-time leaders might be found, because it is very useful for you to have contact with those in a similar position to you. In addition, you should build up your direct contacts and being a member of various networks will help you to do so.

Some people misuse networking and it is important that you use it for the right reason and in the right way. There is nothing worse than someone who tries to network solely out of self-interest. Keep some simple points in mind:

> **"Some people misuse networking."**

▶ Don't seek out contacts solely for what you think you might get out of the relationship.

▶ Take a long-term view of networking. Contacts will prove useful, but rarely overnight.

▶ Be prepared to help your contacts, but don't immediately ask for something in return.

▶ Don't be a name dropper, there is nothing worse.

▶ Networking does not mean handing out your business card to all and sundry.

▶ Be proactive in sustaining your network.

Apart from the formal networks you will build, it goes without saying that maintaining a good social network is important – if only to keep you sane!

Identify mentors to support you in future

You should identify mentors for yourself, both inside and outside your organisation, as you seek to develop your leadership potential. This applies both before you start in the role and whilst in it. Mentoring will be another important support mechanism for you, so use it to its full potential. In particular, mentors can help you with developing your leadership qualities and core skills, but you do need to choose them carefully.

Although such relationships are generally informal, they should be structured and guided by a defined purpose. To this end, consider the following points when seeking to identify mentors:

▶ The mentors you choose should be individuals you know and respect as leaders, or for the specific talents and expertise they possess.

▶ At the outset, discuss how you both view the mentoring relationship developing and agree in general terms the objectives for the relationship.

▶ If each mentoring relationship is to have any concrete value to you, then it must be clearly focused upon specific development needs. You can use the goals you develop here as a starting point.

▶ You should determine the precise areas that each mentor can help you with. Don't think that one mentor can meet all your support needs.

▶ Agree a structured approach and define how often you will meet and so on. Don't leave it to chance – you need to be proactive.

You should also regularly review progress with each mentor – both in achievement of the development needs, but also in terms of how the relationship is developing – to ensure that it remains beneficial and worthwhile to you both. No point in wasting your time and theirs if it is not adding value.

Action

Consider the various networks that will be beneficial to you and identify potential mentors that you can approach. Use the goal-setting framework to make sure you take the necessary steps to make this happen.

Goal 5 – Change, but stay true to yourself

This final goal is a general consideration which applies to all first-time leaders. Whilst it is essential that you address your personal areas for improvement (and you will need to change certain aspects of your behaviour as a leader), it is also imperative that you stamp your own personality on the role. We all adopt a work persona to some degree, but you cannot and should not try to become something you are not. Remember, becoming a leader means adopting a new mindset, not a new personality.

> *" Becoming a leader means adopting a new mindset, not a new personality. "*

First-time leaders often fall into the trap of changing completely once they get appointed. But nothing winds team members up more than this. However, there might be a dilemma facing you in this regard, if you end up taking charge of the team you are currently a member of. If you don't change, then your team might not see you as being in charge, but if you change too much then the team will resent this. There is no easy answer for addressing this issue. Becoming the leader of a team that you were once a member of does require a change, but not too radically and not too quickly. It is a matter of allowing the nature of the relationship to subtly change over time, without making it so obvious that former team members take it as an insult.

Action

This goal may not require specific action on your behalf at this point. But do give some consideration as to how you will redefine past relationships if you are likely to be taking charge of the same team you are currently a member of.

There is no pretence that all the tasks you will identify within these five key goals can be addressed within a short period. As you plan ahead, even if you do not have specific dates for completing certain tasks you identify, you should at least prioritise them into short, medium and long-term actions. But you must ensure that you are proactive in actually doing what you set out to do and review progress regularly. Finally, do not forget to spend time thinking what additional personal goals you may wish to set yourself.

As you get ready to lead, you must:	
Stop	**Start**
Thinking that the leadership mindset should remain in your head	Defining your vision and when you become a leader, communicating it to your team
Hoping that you will someday magically enhance your leadership profile	Taking practical steps now to develop your leadership qualities
Putting off developing your ability to communicate	Becoming a better communicator now

Reflect upon

As you continue on your road to leadership effectiveness, you will need a roadmap to guide your development. The five goals presented here and those that you have developed yourself are intended to provide you with one. When you move ahead, keep the following key messages in mind:

▶ Goals are important; they provide focus for your efforts.

▶ The goal-setting framework allows you to translate the 'big picture' into practical steps to get you there. It also allows you to measure your progress.

▶ The five leadership goals are intended to help you to develop your potential to lead. You will likely have additional goals to add to that list.

▶ A leader needs a vision and you must develop one, so that you can steer your team in the right direction.

▶ Nobody can achieve perfection, but you want to get as close as you can to the ideal leadership profile so that you can be a role model to others.

▶ You need to pay particular attention to improving your levels of self-control, for this impacts heavily on many things you will do as a leader.

▶ Work hard at becoming a better communicator and, in doing so, you will automatically become a stronger leader.

▶ Don't try to do it all alone. Cultivate mentors for support and develop internal and external networks.

▶ Change is required to succeed as a leader but remember to stay true to yourself.

You are now clear on where you need to concentrate your efforts as you get ready to lead. In Part 6, there is a change in emphasis and guidance is offered on what you need to do once you actually start in a leadership role.

Making an Impact

Can you lead in practice?

'The leaders who work most effectively, it seems to me, never say "I". And that's not because they have trained themselves not to say "I". They don't think "I". They think "we"; they think "team". They understand their job to be to make the team function. They accept responsibility and don't sidestep it, but "we" gets the credit ... This is what creates trust, what enables you to get the task done.'

Peter F Drucker
Consultant, Author and Professor, 1909–2005

Our primary focus in this book has been to prepare you for the leadership role. You have considered whether you are made of the right stuff to make it as a leader and you have identified the key skills that will help you to succeed. You should now have translated what you learned about yourself into concrete personal goals to help you to enhance your potential. But you are no doubt eager to see how all of this is going to play out in practice and this will be our focus in this section.

The emphasis here will primarily be in two areas. First, we will look at how you can apply your leadership style using the model developed earlier. This will be achieved by considering how you would address a number of real-life scenarios. Following that, practical issues related to developing your team will be explored using the eight building-blocks.

In Part 6, you will find answers to important questions like:

▶ How are the leadership styles applied in practice?

▶ What should I consider when I start in the leadership role?

▶ What practical steps can I take to build my team?

11

Choosing your leadership style

As you progressed through this book, you should have been watching how leaders in your organisation deal with various situations that arise. What have you noticed so far? Have you seen different styles in action and could you relate them to our model? Leadership is about action and all the models in the world are useless unless you can use them effectively. To help you apply our model, five real-life scenarios are presented here with analyses of how the leader in question addressed the situation and which style was adopted.

Our primary focus will be to discover how you can put into practice what you already know in principle about leadership style. Here is the model again to remind you:

High	◄--►	Low
Direction and Control		
Steering Style	**Engaging Style**	**Facilitating Style**
Involvement and Autonomy		
Low	◄--►	High
Low	**Mutual Trust and Respect**	High

Five scenarios based on actual occurrences in various organisations are described here. Read each scenario first, and think about the questions posed in each case. Don't worry about the exact solution, but simply concentrate upon whether you would adopt a *steering, engaging* or *facilitating* style in dealing with the issue. Then follow the discussion after each one.

Leadership Scenario 1

> ### Scenario 1
>
> A group of employees worked in a warehouse for a large distribution company. Their job was to collect the individual order forms which were printed off from a central database. Once they printed off the order, the employees gathered the items on the list from around the warehouse and assembled them into batches and loaded them on to the relevant delivery trucks. The order form listed items alphabetically, whereas the warehouse storage units were designated by the serial number of the particular item. Following an analysis of customer feedback, it was identified that the orders were filled correctly approximately 90% of the time. The general manager was unhappy about the result and told the warehouse team leader to resolve the issue quickly.

Before you read on, think about the following:

▶ What is the real problem to be addressed here?

▶ If you were the warehouse team leader, what leadership style would you use to resolve this problem?

It is clear that there was a difficulty here, in that 10% of orders were prepared incorrectly to some extent. This of course could not be overlooked and had to be quickly solved as it was impacting negatively on customer satisfaction.

If you were the leader of the team in this case, there is a temptation to immediately adopt the *steering* style whereby you would exercise high direction and control over the development and implementation of the solution. But that may not be the best approach. As the team leader you could devise a solution and simply inform the team, which would be the *steering* style, but you would be overlooking one important point. That being, the team got it right 90% of the time, so they must be doing some things well. As a leader you have to take this into consideration because the team are relatively effective. A better way would be to adopt the *engaging* style first and involve them in the search for the best solution.

In the real situation, the leader met with the team and explained the problem. He also defined clearly the solution he wanted, i.e. 100% accuracy, and asked the team members for suggestions. The team members identified that the order forms did not match the layout of the warehouse, so there was a lot of running back and forth and sometimes things got overlooked. They had mentioned this before, but nobody had taken any notice. Consequently, the layout of the warehouse was reorganised to match as closely as possible the structure of the customer order form and the problem went away quite quickly.

The important point about this, and indeed all the scenarios we will use, is that the leader needs to think through the impact of the style they adopt. If he had adopted the steering style, the team may have felt that they had no input into their work and in any case they had already identified the problem before but nobody had listened. It might have been quicker just to impose a solution, but by adopting an *engaging* approach, the team felt involved and consequently valued to some extent.

> **❝ The leader needs to think through the impact of the style they adopt. ❞**

This is an example of the difference between leadership and management. Leadership always means finding the best solution, not the easiest one. By using this approach, the leader was still retaining the final say over the solution and the outcome he wanted, but the team had a chance to input their ideas.

Key learning points from Scenario 1

▶ When a team is generally performing to a high standard, it is more likely that the leader should involve them in decision-making, or in other words adopt the *engaging* style.

▶ Making the decision for the team, the *steering* style, might be quicker but in this case would cause resentment because the team already knew the problem and the solution but hadn't been listened to.

▶ When teams are involved in devising solutions that directly affect them, they are more likely to make it work, as they feel more ownership towards it than if a solution is imposed.

▶ However, had the percentage of mistaken orders been much higher, say 30/40%, the style adopted by the leader would probably have been more *steering* in nature.

Leadership Scenario 2

Scenario 2

A new team leader was appointed to head a team of 20 designers working in a leading design firm. The previous team leader had been in place for several years and had recently left. Overall, the design team had gained an excellent reputation for creativity and innovation within their industry and had won a number of awards. The new leader, who had previously been a team member, was appointed because he was the longest-serving member of the team and was seen to be next in line.

The new team leader was eager to establish himself quickly and to prove to the team that he could be just as good as his predecessor. One of the areas that he felt required improvement was how the workload was organised and distributed between the team, as he believed that the designers had too much freedom over how they planned their week. The old system had worked well under the previous leader, but the new leader felt that more structure would be good for everyone.

To address this, he introduced a new reporting system, whereby each designer had to provide a work plan at the beginning of every week. Despite protests from the team members, the new leader told them that this was to be the new approach from then on and it wouldn't change, so they should get used to it. In any case, the leader believed that they would see the benefits of this new system over time.

In making these changes, the leader had hoped to further improve the productivity of the team and the overall quality of their work. However, a month after the introduction of the new system, there had been one or two delays in meeting client deadlines, which had rarely occurred before. The team leader felt that this was because a couple of the team members were deliberately slowing down the pace of work. He challenged them about this, which led to a number of heated arguments developing. The departmental head naturally became aware of this and spoke to the team leader about it, indicating that they expected the situation to be resolved quickly as the company could not afford to upset any of its major clients.

Before you read on, consider the following:

▶ How do you think the team leader handled this situation so far?

▶ What style did he adopt?

▶ Did it work?

▶ What might you have done differently?

This scenario is an example of applying the wrong leadership style in a given situation and your thoughts should focus not on whether you agree with the changes made, but rather on whether the approach taken to implement them was effective.

The new leader wanted to exercise more direction and control over the design team and to stamp his authority in the new position. In essence, he was very high on the *steering* style of leadership but in addition somewhat rigid and stubborn in its application. As the new leader, he sought to implement change and establish himself and you can't perhaps blame him for thinking like that, but he got the approach wrong.

In this case, the leader tried to exercise total direction and control (*very high steering style*) over the team with little or no involvement from them, which was radically different from what happened previously. He made no attempt to explain why the changes were beneficial and did little to build bridges with the team. The new leader's style was wrong for a number of reasons:

▶ First, by imposing change on them, the leader in fact created significant resentment, which affected the overall morale of the team and subsequently its performance.

▶ Second, as this was an established team, performing well, they warranted involvement and participation in making decisions about changes. Remember that effective teams do not respond well to very high steering styles of leadership.

The new leader should have encouraged more involvement from the team in determining a new route forward or, at the very least, been willing to explain in greater detail what he was trying to achieve. In other words, he should have adopted the *engaging* style whereby he sat down and explained the rationale for the changes, allowing the team to make some contribution to the decision-making process.

> In the real situation, after continued conflict among the team, the department head had to step in and resolve the situation directly. This naturally affected the standing of the new leader among the team. Unfortunately, the leader didn't learn from the situation and allowed a battle of wills to develop between himself and two team members. This led to a further deterioration of overall relationships between them. In the end, the leader left after six months as he felt under too much pressure.

Key learning points from Scenario 2

▶ As a new team leader, you do need to make your mark, but change should not be introduced too quickly.

❝Change should not be introduced too quickly.❞

▶ When introducing change, you need to consider what level the team are at in terms of effectiveness. A team that is generally effective will not respond well to simply being told what to do.

▶ A leader should always be willing to at least explain their decisions, even if they are not willing, or in a position, to change their mind.

There is another learning point here and it relates to what we said earlier about having some basic attributes that underpin the leadership. The leader in question was appointed because he was next in line, but it quickly became clear that he lacked a leadership profile and the core skills to succeed in the role.

Leadership Scenario 3

Scenario 3

A new leader was appointed as head of the finance team in the corporate office of a large hotel company. She was responsible for a team of accountants, analysts and administration assistants. The previous leader had been in the position for a long time, but had recently retired. The new leader had been with the company for a number of years, working as head accountant in one of the company's hotels.

After taking on the new role, the leader felt there wasn't any need to make changes as the team seemed to be working well, so she mainly just offered support when required. The majority of the team responded well to this and relationships for the most part were initially good. However, after a number of months the leader began to have frequent confrontations with one of the senior accountants, who began to constantly question her decisions, often in front of other members of the team. In order not to lose face, the leader 'met fire with fire' on the occasions when this individual challenged her. At first, the leader felt that this person was just being difficult, but over time she noticed that others in the team also began to adopt similar approaches.

Before you read on, consider the following:

▶ What is the problem facing the new leader?

▶ How did she deal with it?

▶ What are your thoughts on the leadership style she adopted?

This is a complex situation and there are no easy answers but the new leader did make some important mistakes. Whereas in Scenario 2, the new leader adopted a *steering* style in an effort to establish himself, this leader did the opposite. At the beginning she adopted the *facilitating* style, where she exercised little direction or control over the team. This was a mistake, for although the team was performing well, it is still important for a new leader to establish her authority.

A better approach would have been to use a mix of the *low steering or engaging* style for the first few months. Initially, the new leader needed to outline her vision and explain to the team what her expectations were of their behaviour and performance. In short, she should have provided more direction and control over the team than she actually did. As a result of this lack of direction, the more senior members began challenging her position, which often happens.

But it is in her response to this that the new leader made the biggest mistake. By being seen to openly confront this individual, and by responding to their aggression, the new leader in effect 'conditioned' others in the team that this is how things now work in the department. Of course, she should have dealt with the difficult team member, because it was essential to do so. But she needed to remain in control of her own reactions, as well as not doing it in front of the whole team every time. The first time she was challenged in an unacceptable way, the leader should have spoken to the relevant individual, making it clear that their approach was unacceptable. In other words, she should have taken a *high steering* approach with that person. Instead, she responded with aggression, which only made the situation worse.

Key learning points from Scenario 3

▶ When you take charge of an established team who are performing well, it is still important to establish yourself as the leader at the early stages, but this does not mean being very high on the steering style. It can be a mix of steering/engaging and this can simply mean sitting down with the team and defining your expectations and listening to any concerns they may have.

▶ With different individuals in a team, it will often be necessary to adopt different styles. When a team member acts or behaves in an unacceptable manner, it is essential to confront this immediately, but not in an aggressive manner and not in front of the team. *Steering*, in this case, means sitting the individual down and making it very clear that their behaviour will not be tolerated. You are prepared to listen and discuss matters with them, but only when they address you in an appropriate manner.

▶ As a leader, aggression should not be part of your toolkit for it only breeds resentment, fear and usually encourages aggressive responses from stronger members in the team. You might lose your temper on the odd occasion, but don't make it a feature of your approach.

▶ A leader must clearly set out for the team what the acceptable norms of behaviour are as part of their vision. When someone crosses the line, the leader must deal with it as soon as it occurs, for to ignore it runs the risk of sending out the message that it is acceptable. This can then encourage others to test the waters.

Leadership Scenario 4

Scenario 4

A team of men working as baggage handlers at an airport were expected to wear special ear defenders to protect them from hearing damage due to the noise from the planes. The company had regularly stated that it was mandatory to wear them at all times. Despite this, many of the employees did not, or at best only wore them when a team leader was around.

The team leader put up notices and sent memos to all employees emphasising the importance of the ear defenders and warning of disciplinary action for those who failed to wear them.

The situation did not improve and the team leader was told by his boss to resolve the matter quickly. Fearing for his own position, the team leader immediately warned the team that anyone caught not wearing the ear defenders would be disciplined. This had little effect and a number of team members then received written warnings. Despite this, the team continued to wear them when the team leader was around, but rarely when he wasn't.

After two team members were dismissed for failing to wear the ear defenders as required, a major dispute arose at the company. In seeking to resolve the dispute, it transpired that the reason that the team members did not wear the ear defenders in practice was that when working close to planes, they could not hear each other's instructions, so they had to lift them off every couple of minutes. In the end, the company bought head sets with inbuilt microphones which solved the problem.

Before you read on, consider the following:

▶ What was the problem facing the leader?

▶ How did he deal with it?

▶ What are your thoughts on the leadership style he has adopted?

This case shows the impact of poor communication between a leader and his team and the prolonged effects of a lack of leadership. First of all, this is a health and safety issue, so the company were right to be concerned about it. The team leader continuously adopted a *high steering* style, but was also quite aggressive in his approach. When this failed, he disciplined any offenders.

At no time was there any meaningful communication with the team; in other words, *engaging* styles were never used. Now it might seem incredible that this could go so far but it happened because the team leader and the company in general did not engage the employees at any level. It was a case of 'them and us' and they only really communicated when they had to resolve disputes. If the *engaging* style had been used earlier by the team leader, this specific issue might have been resolved without causing so much acrimony.

Key learning points from Scenario 4

▶ This scenario emphasises the need for communication and highlights what happens in its absence.

▶ Leaders sometimes have to make unpopular decisions or enforce important regulations but that does not mean they should never listen to the viewpoints of team members.

▶ Being prepared to listen is not a sign of weakness, but of strength. Sitting down with the team regularly allows for a two-way flow of opinions. In this case, it would have meant avoidance of a dispute.

"Being prepared to listen is not a sign of weakness, but of strength."

▶ It is important to remember that the benefits to be attained from communication are only seen over a period of time. One-offs don't add much value, so you need to communicate regularly with your team.

Leadership Scenario 5

Scenario 5

A new leader was appointed to oversee a team of reservationists working for a large travel company. The work of the department involved handling enquiries and taking reservation bookings for clients. When she started, the new leader sat with the team members and outlined her expectations and also addressed some concerns the team had about aspects of the job. Since then, the team generally worked well and the leader had not had any major staffing issues to deal with. However, one problem arose unexpectedly which caused significant difficulties.

One of the girls, the longest-serving and best member of the team, began taking unscheduled breaks usually towards the end of the day. She was never gone too long but the leader felt it wasn't acceptable just to disappear like that. Upon speaking to her about it, the employee explained that when she had completed her workload for the day, she did pop out for an occasional smoke. In any case, she 'did a lot more work than the others so she deserved it and anyway it wasn't affecting anyone else'. The team leader emphasised that it wasn't permissible to take unscheduled breaks because if she allowed her to do it, then everyone would end up expecting the same. If she had finished her workload for the day, there were other things that could be done. But despite this chat, the leader noticed that this girl continued to take unscheduled breaks occasionally.

The leader tried the engaging approach again, hoping to come to a reasonable agreement but the team member remained obstinate. So the leader explained that she would no longer tolerate the unscheduled breaks and the team member reluctantly agreed to stop taking them. But different problems later arose. Due to not getting her way, the girl's performance dropped and she became slower at her work. Over time, she became more and more difficult and despite the best efforts of the leader in trying to reason with her, nothing seemed to work. Eventually, this led to disciplinary action being taken with the girl and ended in her leaving the company of her own accord.

Before you read on, consider the following:

▶ What was the problem facing the new leader?

▶ How did she deal with it?

▶ What are your thoughts on the leadership style she adopted?

Like all leadership problems at work, there are rarely perfect solutions. On the one hand, it would be nice to be flexible with a good employee, but on the other it is not possible to have separate rules for each team member. In this case, the team leader began with an *engaging* style in seeking to resolve the situation through discussion. But this didn't work. Then she moved to a more *steering* style and defined for the team member what solution was acceptable, i.e. no unscheduled breaks. The particular team member didn't like this and eventually left.

What was really behind this issue was that the girl in question had applied for the leader's position but had been overlooked. The leader who was appointed did try a number of approaches, but the girl could never get over her resentment towards the company. Sometimes there is no alternative but to lose a disgruntled team member when all other approaches fail. It is a shame when this happens, but a worse case scenario is having every member of the team thinking they can set their own terms, even over what seems like a relatively minor issue. If this girl had been allowed more breaks than everyone else, it would only have been a matter of time until other team members started to look for special terms of some kind. A lot of employees feel they work harder than others, so where do you draw the line?

Key learning points from Scenario 5

▶ This scenario shows that it's never easy to lead people and even when a leader tries to do the right things, it doesn't always work. But the leader did try to deal with the problem in the correct way and that is the key.

▶ The leader did adopt a number of approaches, but personal resentment lay behind the problem and you may encounter similar situations. All you can do is deal with it in as professional a manner as possible.

▶ Sometimes having tried everything reasonable, there is no alternative but to lose an unhappy team member even when they are a strong performer. If the attitude is not right, then being a good at the job is not enough. You need both.

Applying your style in practice

These five scenarios should demonstrate the need for you to 'think' as much as to 'act' when you become a leader. Leading people is rarely trouble-free and many situations will arise which require significant analysis before acting – often this has to be done under pressure. The scenarios also highlight that flexibility in your approach will be essential and applying the best leadership style to fit the needs of the situation will be a challenge. There is unfortunately no simple formula that can serve as a guide for all occasions. However, as a rule, you should try to adopt an engaging style with your team for as much of the time as possible once you have established yourself with your team.

These scenarios also show that much of your time at work will be taken up in dealing with people-related issues as you strive to ensure that outcomes are achieved. That is why the leadership profile and the core leadership skills are so important. Without working on developing your potential through achieving your personal goals, then the application of any leadership styles will become extremely difficult for you. It is not so much the style that you will adopt which is important, but whether you have the personal capacity or skills to carry it off.

Another point is evident here. As we said earlier, the idea promoted about leadership being concerned with the transforming hero seeking to change the world is clearly not the reality for most first-time leaders in the workplace. That is why we have tried throughout this book to place leadership at work in the right context. Leading people at work can be exciting, challenging and rewarding, but it often has to focus on the ordinary and less stimulating aspects of getting the job done well. That does not mean that the leader's role is mundane, but some of the things you will have to do are.

As a general rule, when you start in your leadership role, you will tend to adopt the steering style of leadership during the early days. You want your team members to understand where you are coming from and what you expect from them. You will also need to define what the acceptable behaviours are. This requires direction and control on your behalf until you get the team operating in the way that you want. Once you see that they are progressing, then you can shift to a more engaging style.

But don't think that, even at the start, you will only use the steering style, although this will likely be your predominant approach in the first few weeks. You need to judge the best response to each situation as it arises.

> **You need to judge the best response to each situation as it arises.**

As a leader, you must:	
Stop	**Start**
Acting first, then thinking	Thinking about the best approach before you act
Believing that one leadership style will fit all occasions	Understanding that flexibility in your leadership style will be key
Worrying when you get the approach wrong	Learning from the experience and aiming to be better next time

12

CHAPTER TWELVE

Building your team

Based on what you learned from the earlier exercise on teams, how is your current team performing? Would you describe it as a good team? What tells you that it is? If things are working well, try to figure out why, so that you can use that to your advantage in future. If it isn't, make sure you don't make the same mistakes.

All great leaders think teams, not groups. In fact they don't just think about them, they energetically build and sustain them. The quality of your team will play a big part in your success, so make sure you get it right. The practical measures that you can take to build your team are our concern here and along the way we will deal with what you need to do to make an impact as a leader. It is impossible to provide precise timelines for the actions described, but broad priorities and deadlines are indicated.

> *All great leaders think teams, not groups.*

Setting your priorities

One of the most common concerns for first-time leaders is how long they have to make an impact in the role. You are probably looking for an answer to this question specified in terms of weeks or months. Unfortunately, there is no set timeline because it depends on your organisation, your boss and indeed yourself. Whatever the precise timeframe, you will understand that it is not indefinite. So, you will have to set things up early in order to show worthwhile results as quickly as you can.

One way to approach planning your early days as leader is to take your first six months as being the critical landmark and examine what are the key milestones within that time block. You can then prioritise the necessary actions.

Immediate Action	Early Priority	Condition-led
Day 1 to end of Month 1	1–3 months	3–6 months and beyond

1 *Immediate Action* – Things you will need to be thinking about or doing at the very early stages. The seeds if you like.

2 *Early Priority* – As your relationship with your team grows, you will then build upon the seeds you have already sown.

3 *Condition-led* – Depending upon how the team is progressing, you will have to determine the appropriate timescale for further action.

These three categories will be useful in helping you to prioritise what you will have to do during your early days as leader. In some cases, it may be possible for you to make a noticeable impact quite early on, but in reality you will have to put measures in place at the beginning which will later materialise into positive outcomes and benefits. But you will need to do this groundwork and not just be swept along by the day-to-day pressures. For this to happen, you need a plan.

Early days in the role

There are a number of general considerations that you should keep in mind, as they will greatly influence your ability to get results later on.

1 *Clarify your role*

One of your first actions should be to sit down with your boss and define very clearly their expectations from you regarding your performance. You should seek to agree specific objectives, priorities, timelines and performance measures so that both parties are clear on what is required.

2 *Analyse the situation*

Your first couple of weeks should be seen as a period to 'look and learn'. You should focus on getting to know the business (if you don't already know it), your team and their individual personalities. It is not a time for change, as you should not make the mistake of making changes too quickly, as this is likely to backfire.

3 *Get to know your team members*

A priority for you should be to get to know your team members as individuals. Some of this will be achieved simply by working with them on a day-to-day basis and through casual observance. However, you should also sit with them individually to define their expectations, motivations and concerns regarding their role. Even if you already know them, keep an eye out for how they are reacting to your promotion.

> **❝ Get to know your team members as individuals. ❞**

4 *Relationship building*

This is a critical time for defining relationships with your boss, the team, your colleagues and mentors. You set the tone here for the future and you need to build strong relationships from day one.

5 *Building respect*

Remember, just as you are judging the situation, so too are your team, and they are making assessments about what they think of you. You need to be on the ball from the start, because you won't get a second chance to make a good first impression. This is where many of the personal qualities we discussed earlier come into play and you must show people by your behaviour what type of person you are and what type of leader you are going to be. You therefore need to demonstrate quickly that you are committed, confident, up to speed with the job and willing to be open and communicative with your team.

6 *Identifying issues, problems and opportunities*

At the early stages, you should be consciously identifying the issues, problems and opportunities that you will address at a later point. Although you shouldn't make changes too early, you should be thinking of 'small wins' – improvements you can implement that will make a difference and get you noticed.

7 *Develop a plan*

At the end of the first month, you should prepare a plan outlining what you propose to do across a range of dimensions. This should be communicated to your boss and your team as appropriate. To your boss, this will be a sign that you are proactive and to your team it shows that you are in control.

These early considerations are important, so do not overlook them. Now, let's get more specific and examine what you will have to do to start building your team.

Building a successful team – action plans

The eight building-blocks of teams should serve to guide your actions when you start in the leadership role and you must consider what needs to be done for each. Whether you are taking on a new team or the one you used to be a member of, the principles are exactly the same.

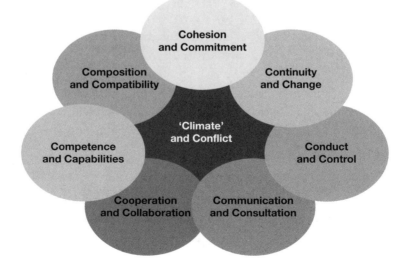

Here we will examine the practical actions to be taken within each building-block. You will find:

▶ A 'snapshot' of what you should do, offering clear objectives and definite actions within the three timeframes mentioned earlier

▶ Some tips to guide your efforts.

As we have done throughout this book, we will focus on the leadership-related issues concerning building your team. You should not forget that you will also have to learn and implement many new job-related tasks as well.

Building-block 1 – cohesion and commitment

Teams cannot be effective unless everyone is pulling in the same direction and one of your immediate concerns will be to focus on developing cohesion and commitment within the team.

Cohesion & Commitment - Snapshot		
Your Objectives		
▶ *Ensure that all team members fully understand and are committed to your 'vision' for the team* ▶ *Create a process to define common goals and to ensure that you get 'buy-in' from all team members*		
Actions Required		
Immediate Action	**Early Priority**	**Condition-led**
▶ Hold a team meeting to explain and clarify your 'vision' ▶ Get to know each team member on a one-to-one basis	▶ Once settled in, create a process to jointly define and agree common team goals	▶ Review the common goals regularly with your team ▶ Proactively address issues that arise which affect cohesion and commitment ▶ Deal with individuals who do not share the common goals

Some tips

- ▶ Communicate your vision to your team at an early point.
- ▶ At a later stage, you must work with the team to define some common goals:
  - ▶ You will not necessarily have to end up with a written set of common goals, some teams do it that way, some do not.
  - ▶ Whatever approach you take, everyone in the team will need to have a clear understanding of what you are collectively trying to achieve.
  - ▶ The common goals can be centred on issues such as having high levels of trust and honesty, good openness and communication, mutual respect and support and so on.
  - ▶ Review the common goals regularly with the team at monthly team meetings.
- ▶ Devote time during the early stages of your appointment to sit with each team member on a one-to-one basis to discuss how they feel about their role.
- ▶ By doing so you are seeking to get to know them as individuals in order to assess the different personalities with your team.
- ▶ You cannot hope to motivate an individual without understanding them.
- ▶ Even if you were promoted from within, you should still do this because it will give you an indication as to how team members are reacting to your appointment.

Building-block 2 – composition and compatibility

The composition and compatibility of your team are important from the point of view of day-to-day relationships and overall team

❝ Build a team that has the right mix of abilities and personalities. ❞

effectiveness. Naturally you will not be in a position to influence this immediately, if the team is already in place, but you should over the longer term seek to build a team that has the right mix of abilities and personalities.

Composition & Compatibility- Snapshot		
Your Objectives		
▶ *Ensure that the mix in your team is right, comprising individuals and personalities that represent the best fit* ▶ *When the need arises, ensure that you recruit the most suitable candidates for your team*		
Actions Required		
Immediate Action	Early Priority	Condition-led
▶ When outlining your vision, emphasise the importance of teamwork, mutual trust and support ▶ Monitor team performance and highlight issues/ individuals that may need to be dealt with at a later stage	▶ Act as a coach where there are compatibility issues between team members ▶ Identify any potential blockages in team performance	▶ Develop and use employee profiles as part of recruitment ▶ Only recruit individuals who fit with existing members ▶ Consider holding occasional teambuilding events to address compatibility issues identified

Some tips

▶ As part of your vision you should describe what you want to see from the team in terms of their interactions.

▶ In the early stages devote considerable attention to the team dynamic.

▶ Try to identify where there may be compatibility issues.

▶ Where problems are identified that warrant attention, deal with them early.

▶ Take a coaching approach in dealing with individuals or situations that do not meet your expectations in terms of team compatibility.

▶ Consider organising occasional teambuilding events that seek to identify and address barriers that may be affecting team effectiveness.

▶ You will need to work through others to achieve this, such as the HR department, but your role should always be to make a strong case for enhancing the capabilities of your team as a unit.

▶ Providing your team with training in 'how to be a better team' can dramatically improve internal communication and interaction and hence overall effectiveness.

▶ In the longer term, ensure that you give the recruitment of new team members significant attention.

Building-block 3 – competence and capabilities

As you get to know your team members, you should also be assessing their competence and capabilities. This simply involves observing how they perform their work and discussing their training needs with them. You should seek to identify those who are underperforming as well as those individuals who show potential and are eager to progress up the ranks.

Competence & Capabilities - Snapshot		
Your Objectives		
▶ Ensure that all team members have the competences required to do the work to standard ▶ Develop those individuals who show potential and are eager to progress		
Actions Required		
Immediate Action	Early Priority	Condition-led
▶ Consider individual strengths and weaknesses in relation to competence ▶ Identify high performers who are eager to progress	▶ Provide training, coaching and other support to team members who are not at the required level of competence	▶ Use coaching in a wider developmental context ▶ Delegate responsibilities to those who are willing and able for it

Some tips

▶ Spend significant time during the early stages monitoring individual performance so that you know where their strengths and weaknesses lie.

▶ Constantly provide training and development for your team.

▶ Be a coach and continuously search for opportunities where you can develop individuals within your team.

▶ Use delegation, but choose those whom you will delegate to very carefully.

Sometimes leaders can be short-sighted with regard to coaching and indeed delegation. They often avoid developing certain team members, because although they can see their potential, they are afraid that one day this individual might outshine them. This is a mistake. Preventing high-potential team members from developing will lead to resentment and in any case the better ones will move on in search of better opportunities they seek. The trick here is always to develop such individuals as you will see a lot of positives in return, but to be continuously enhancing your own skills and knowledge so that you maintain the performance gap in your favour.

In addition, your team as a unit will need certain capabilities to allow them to operate effectively as a unit. Teams often need support to enhance their potential and you should be aware that blockages can emerge which will impact on effectiveness. This can be as simple as certain team members not feeling comfortable in opening up with each other, or having difficulties in collective problem-solving or decision-making. Your role as a team leader will be to constantly identify any blockages and where problems do arise, you will have to take appropriate action.

Building-block 4 – cooperation and collaboration

It is an obvious requirement that teams must cooperate and collaborate if they wish to achieve their goals. What is not so obvious is that you can enhance these areas by the actions you take.

Cooperation & Collaboration - Snapshot		
Your Objectives		
▶ Take proactive steps to enhance the levels of cooperation in the team ▶ Use collaborative approaches to problem-solving where possible		
Actions Required		
Immediate Action	**Early Priority**	**Condition-led**
▶ Monitor the levels of cooperation between team members ▶ Identify areas where team cooperation can be improved	▶ Be conscious in how you allocate the workload. Try to ensure that the same people don't always end up working together. Mix and match it!	▶ Establish teams to focus on specific problems and make suggestions/ recommendations

Some tips

▶ Find out if there are cliques within the team.

▶ Over time, work to break these up, but do so slowly and subtly.

▶ Try where possible to ensure that the work is allocated in such a way that the same people don't end up working together all the time.

▶ This encourages the wider development of relationships within the team and can help to improve overall cooperation over time.

▶ In particular, when different projects arise, this provides you with an opportunity to put this principle into action and you should pay particular attention to how you build project teams to ensure the mix is right.

Building-block 5 – communication and consultation

Informal communication is a natural part of the workplace, but as a leader you should develop structured communication processes which are rigidly adhered to. Formal communications at work should always have a twin focus – to discuss matters relating to the outcomes and to address issues relating to the team. As such, you should try to have a consultative aspect to all your communications with your team. In addition, where possible, communication should be face to face and written forms should be kept to a minimum and used to reinforce matters already discussed, as opposed to being the main vehicle for transmitting a message. Avoid at all costs the memo or email culture as the primary forms of interacting with your team.

« Where possible, communication should be face to face. »

Communication & Consultation - Snapshot

Your Objectives
▶ *Establish high levels of structured, formal communication with your team* ▶ *Consult frequently with your team on work-related matters*

Actions Required		
Immediate Action	**Early Priority**	**Condition-led**
▶ Introduce daily briefings, if not already in place	▶ Introduce a monthly team meeting with a structured agenda	▶ Adopt a consultative approach through using the 'engaging' style of leadership as often as possible

Some tips

▶ Work consistently on developing your own communication skills.

▶ Introduce daily briefings and make sure that you stick to them.

▶ Hold a monthly meeting with your team.

▶ Have a set agenda and allow them to contribute points to it in advance.

▶ Make sure these meetings are structured and effective.

▶ Do not allow any one individual to dominate the discussion during these meetings.

▶ Always be prepared to listen to the ideas and opinions of your team.

▶ Even when you don't adopt the approach they would like, be willing to explain why.

▶ Ensure that action agreed at these meetings is followed up.

Here are some tips for making your meetings more effective:

Before the meeting
Consider:
▶ What is the purpose of the meeting/What do I want to achieve?
▶ Who actually needs to be there?
▶ What is the most appropriate time to hold the meeting?
▶ Where is the best place to hold the meeting?
▶ What will be discussed – the agenda?
▶ Ensure that everyone attending is clear on what will and won't be discussed

During the Meeting
▶ Start on time. Don't reward latecomers by waiting.
▶ Follow a clear structure: *Introduction, Main Body, Conclusion*
Introduction
▶ Greeting & welcome
▶ State the purpose/time of the meeting
▶ Outline the agenda points
▶ Encourage participation – through you!
▶ Emphasise time constraints
▶ Allocate responsibilities, i.e. note taker/timekeeper
Main Body
You should introduce each agenda point, making initial points for discussion. As discussion takes place it is up to you to:
▶ Maintain control/participation
▶ Keep the discussion on track
▶ Allow involvement from all participants
▶ Prevent conflict from getting out of hand
▶ Keep to allocated time
▶ Summarise agreement/action on each agenda point before moving to next
Conclusion
▶ Finish on time
▶ You should summarise all the points agreed
▶ Ensure that each participant is clear on the action they must take following the meeting and the completion date for same
▶ Thank everyone for attending and for participating
▶ Remind any latecomers on the necessity for arriving on time in future

After the Meeting
▶ Minutes are not required, just action points. What, by when, by whom etc.
▶ You should follow up and make sure that each individual allocated responsibilities/tasks at the meeting actually completes these
▶ It is also useful to discuss with the participants how they felt the meeting went. Feedback is always useful – even if you don't like what you hear – as it helps to make the next one better

Building-block 6 – conduct and control

One of the early challenges for you when taking over a team will be to establish what patterns of behaviour are going to be acceptable. The trick here will be to achieve this without sounding like a parent or schoolteacher and a good time to do it is at the early stage when you are outlining your vision for the team.

Conduct & Control - Snapshot		
Your Objectives		
▶ *Ensure that all team members understand the accepted norms of behaviour* ▶ *Ensure that all team members adhere to them continuously*		
Actions Required		
Immediate Action	**Early Priority**	**Condition-led**
▶ As part of outlining your vision, describe the acceptable behaviours	▶ When individuals don't adhere to these norms, you need to address it at an early point	▶ Individuals who consistently fail to respond in this regard must be dealt with appropriately

Some tips

When individuals display behaviours that are contrary to your vision for the team or, even worse, participate in actions that are unfair or discriminatory to others, you will need to step in very quickly. Some points to consider in approaching this:

▶ When it is something that relates to the team overall, use your daily briefings or monthly meetings to reinforce that it is unacceptable and will not be tolerated.

▶ When it is related to a particular individual, deal directly with them.

▶ You will have to be quite firm in getting the message across that you are not going to allow that behaviour to continue.

▶ With all such matters, you are initially prepared to be open and discuss it (*engaging style*) with the individual in question.

▶ When you do not see improvement, you need to become more direct and you will end up specifying what the team member must do in future (*steering style*).

When you see improvement as a result, you should of course also acknowledge it. If they persist in acting in the unacceptable way, then you may have to move towards disciplinary action.

Building-block 7 – continuity and change

It is clear that as a first-time leader, you will not be in a position to change the world and nor will you be expected to. However, don't let this be an excuse that prevents you from changing the things you can. Equally, never suggest changes just for the sake of it and don't make any serious changes until you have established yourself in your new position.

Continuity & Change - Snapshot		
Your Objectives		
▶ *Continuously strive to find better ways of doing things that improve the quality of outcomes, team morale and motivation* ▶ *Handle all change in an open and transparent manner*		
Actions Required		
Immediate Action	Early Priority	Condition-led
▶ Don't make significant changes too soon; look and learn first	▶ Identify areas where you can create 'small wins' – changes that will make a positive impact and show that you are adding value	▶ View change as a continuous process and always seek to involve your team in decision-making around change where possible

Some tips

- ▶ You should always be on the look-out for better ways of doing things.

- ▶ Even though the level of some changes within your control may be minor, if they lead to improved team performance and better results, then they are worthwhile and will get you noticed.

- ▶ After your first month, you should be clear on where positive changes can be introduced. Have a plan to address them.

- ▶ You should begin to implement them, so that you can see benefits within a reasonable period of time.

- ▶ Try to identify worthwhile changes that can create 'small wins' for you and this will give you confidence to handle larger change issues.

- ▶ Where possible, try to involve your team in the change process as much as you can.

- ▶ Sometimes they can be fully involved from the start, but other times it is your call and they have to live with it. Even in those circumstances, be willing to explain the rationale behind your decision.

Finally, when the team does rise to the challenge of coping with change, no matter how painful the process was in getting there, you should always acknowledge their efforts and recognise their response, as this will help with the next change that comes along.

Building-block 8 – climate and conflict

Depending upon how you address the earlier building-blocks, you will end up with a team that has a healthy climate and team spirit, or one that has significant levels of conflict.

Climate & Conflict - Snapshot		
Your Objectives		
▶ *Ensure that the overall climate within the team is as positive as possible* ▶ *Handle conflict in a proactive manner*		
Actions Required		
Immediate Action	**Early Priority**	**Condition-led**
▶ Put in place the measures described in the other building-blocks such as outlining your vision, communication processes etc.	▶ Open up lines of communication with your team and stick to them ▶ Identify individual motivations, and start working to meet them ▶ Deal with any destructive conflict that arises at an early point	▶ Encourage a social dimension to your team ▶ Use your monthly team meetings to openly discuss motivational issues that relate to the team

Some tips

▶ Constantly monitor the climate within your team.

▶ Address blockages as soon as you identify them.

▶ Make sure you do not inhibit constructive conflict, but do control it.

▶ Develop your own ability to resolve conflict with others.

▶ Deal with all destructive conflict early; do not allow such situations to fester.

▶ Play a mediation type role first, failing that you must impose the solution you expect and monitor compliance with it.

Much of the work required in building your team will take time to implement. You now have some clear guidelines as to what you need to do and when to do it. As a conclusion to this chapter, you should give some more thought now as to some of the priority actions you will take under the eight building-blocks:

Action	
Building-block	**Priority Actions**
Cohesion & Commitment	
Composition & Compatibility	
Competence & Capabilities	
Cooperation & Collaboration	
Communication & Consultation	
Conduct & Control	
Continuity & Change	
Climate & Conflict	

As a leader you must:	
Stop	**Start**
Thinking that developing a winning team just happens	Taking specific action under the eight building-blocks
Hoping your new team can read your mind	Communicating your vision of the future to your team now
Ignoring conflict because it is difficult to deal with	Dealing with all destructive conflict as soon as it emerges

Reflect upon

When you start in a leadership role, you will have lots to do. The content here will provide you with direction for your efforts. You should grasp the leadership challenge early and the more effort you put in at the beginning, the greater the rewards you will see later. As you do so, keep the following key messages in mind:

▶ The need for you to 'think' as much as to 'act' when leading others is at the heart of success.

▶ Leading people is a great opportunity for you, rarely trouble-free, but if you learn to analyse each situation as it arises, you will succeed.

▶ You need to be flexible in your approach and apply the right leadership style to fit the needs of the situation .

▶ Much of your time at work will be taken up dealing with people-related issues as you strive to ensure that outcomes are achieved.

▶ It is not so much the style that you adopt that is important, but whether you have the personal capacity or potential to carry that style off.

▶ When you start, you will need to adopt the steering style more of the time to establish yourself as leader.

▶ You will move to a more engaging style when you feel the team is on track. But even in the early days you have to judge what approach is best in every situation.

▶ Your early days in the leader's role will be critical. Be prepared and make a positive first impression.

▶ Clearly define the expectations of your boss at the very outset.

▶ Define the action required within each of the eight building-blocks according to the three categories.

▶ Categorise your actions into: *Immediate Action*, *Early Priority* and *Condition-led*.

▶ Communicate your vision to your team early, incorporating all the relevant points, and proactively strive to get strong cohesion and commitment within the team.

▶ Identify small wins that you can introduce to raise your profile and credibility.

▶ Monitor closely the motivation levels and team spirit within the team.

It will take time to feel comfortable in the role, so be prepared at the beginning to feel a little lost, but that will pass quickly. Leading teams can be fun, don't forget that. Try to make a little impact every day and the collective effects of this will quickly show.

Looking ahead

We have come to the end of our journey together, but you must now move forward from here, both in continuing to prepare yourself for the leadership position and in making an impact when you get there. It is important not to lose sight of the great opportunity facing you, for being a leader will prove very rewarding and it will open many doors for you in future. In fact, the sky is the limit, if you continuously develop your ability to lead.

If you are to take anything from this book, you should recognise that the future is in your own hands. You have the power to determine the type of leader you become and there will be a direct correlation between your success and the amount of effort you put in. Forget about the notion that your past will determine your future and understand that no one but yourself can stop you becoming a great leader.

When we started down the road together, there were certainly many things you already knew about leadership. It was obvious to you that moving into the leadership role was going to present you with important challenges. You knew that taking responsibility for others was not going to be easy and that you would face many people-related problems. How to deal with them effectively should be even clearer to you now. Along the way, we also addressed many issues that you may not have been aware of. In particular, you probably didn't realise the depth of self-analysis and personal development required as you prepare to lead others. The need for you to build your leadership mindset and profile should now have moved into the known column. So too should the core leadership skills that you will have to master to help you excel as a leader.

There are still plenty of things you may not yet know, for leadership is a journey of discovery and not every situation that may arise can be predicted. However, we have addressed many of the common problems that you will encounter, so you are now well placed to tackle anything that might present itself. The rest will come with time and experience.

&& Leadership is a journey of discovery. &&

We have intentionally highlighted the many challenges you will face as a leader, but you should not fear what lies ahead, but rather move forward fully prepared with realistic expectations. It isn't an easy road and we haven't described it as such, but the rewards are great, for the world of work is crying out for effective leaders. For all the ground we have covered, the journey ahead remains as challenging as it is exciting. But you now have a clear roadmap to guide you. The progress you make will depend on you and your willingness to apply the learning from this book.

As you continue to get ready to lead, you should:

- *Build your leadership mindset* – The more you think like a leader, the easier the rest will be.
- *Enhance your leadership profile* – The stronger your leadership profile, the more you will behave like a leader.
- *Develop your leadership skills* – The better you master the skills, the smoother the transition into leadership will be.
- *Achieve your personal goals* – The more you succeed in your preparations, the more you are preparing to succeed.

We have continuously emphasised the need for you to be proactive in getting yourself ready to lead. After you finish reading this book, don't just set your best intentions aside. Finalise your personal goals and start working to achieve them, reviewing your progress at four-week intervals. Even better, find yourself a mentor now to help you to keep on track. Rome wasn't built in a day as the saying goes, but they did a little bit every day until it was finished.

When you start in the role, you should:

- *Be prepared and focused* so that you can make a good first impression. That will be half the battle.

▶ *Have a plan and follow it*. People like achievers and this will resonate strongly with your boss and the team.

▶ *Be confident and self-assured*. Image is important and if you project an assured air, those around you will be influenced by that.

▶ *Get yourself noticed by your boss, team and colleagues*. Put measures in place early, so that you can show results quickly.

Once in a leadership position, allow a short period of time at the end of each day, week and month to ask yourself: Did I act like an effective leader? What did I do well? What must I do better next time? There will undoubtedly be a few bumps along the way, both in preparing for the role and once you get there. Don't let them dishearten you. You will make mistakes, but don't make the same one twice. You won't always handle every situation in the ideal way. Learn from it and be better next time.

❝ What must I do better next time?❞

As you move ahead, do remember to reward yourself when you achieve a personal goal or something that you set out to do. This helps with future self-motivation. Also, maintain a positive and enjoyable life outside of work. Put your heart and soul into becoming a great leader, but leave your troubles and concerns behind when you finish each day and whatever free time you do have, use it well.

Finally, one last thing – enjoy the journey and best of luck.

Index